T0332415

Nordic Animation

This book examines the state of the animation industry within the Nordic countries. It looks at the success of popular brands such as Moomins and the *Angry Birds*, studios such as Anima Vitae and Qvisten, and individuals from the Nordics who have made their mark on the global animation industry.

This book begins with some historical findings, before moving to recount stories of some of the most well-known Nordic animation brands. A section on Nordic animation studios examines the international success of these companies and its impact on the global animation industry. This book is forward-thinking in scope and places these stories within the context of what the future holds for the Nordic animation industry.

This book will be of great interest to those in the fields of animation and film studies, as well as those with a general interest in Nordic animation.

Liisa Vähäkylä is the Executive Director at Finnanimation—the network of Finnish animation producers—and an independent animation scholar.

Focus Animation

The **Focus Animation Series** aims to provide unique, accessible content that may not otherwise be published. We allow researchers, academics, and professionals the ability to quickly publish high impact, current literature in the field of animation for a global audience. This series is a fine complement to the existing, robust animation titles available through CRC Press/Focal Press.

Series Editor Chris Robinson is the Artistic Director of the Ottawa International Animation Festival (OIAF) and is a well-known figure in the animated film world. We welcome any submissions to help grow the wonderful content we are striving to provide to the animation community.

Nordic Animation
Balancing the East and the West

Liisa Vähäkylä

CRC Press
Taylor & Francis Group
Boca Raton London New York

CRC Press is an imprint of the
Taylor & Francis Group, an informa business

First edition published 2023
by CRC Press
6000 Broken Sound Parkway NW, Suite 300, Boca Raton, FL 33487-2742

by CRC Press
4 Park Square, Milton Park, Abingdon, Oxon, OX14 4RN

CRC Press is an imprint of Taylor & Francis Group, LLC

© 2023 Liisa Vähäkylä

Library of Congress Cataloging-in-Publication Data
Names: Vähäkylä, Liisa, author.
Title: Nordic animation : balancing the East and the West / Liisa Vähäkylä.
Description: Boca Raton : CRC Press, 2023. |
Series: Focus animation series | Includes bibliographical references and index.
Identifiers: LCCN 2022043134 (print) | LCCN 2022043135 (ebook) |
ISBN 9781032149158 (hardback) | ISBN 9781032149172 (paperback) |
ISBN 9781003241737 (ebook)
Subjects: LCSH: Animated film industry–Scandinavia.
Classification: LCC NC1766.S34 V34 2023 (print) | LCC NC1766.S34 (ebook) |
DDC 384/.80948–dc23/eng/20220921
LC record available at https://lccn.loc.gov/2022043134
LC ebook record available at https://lccn.loc.gov/2022043135

ISBN: 9781032149158 (hbk)
ISBN: 9781032149172 (pbk)
ISBN: 9781003241737 (ebk)

DOI: 10.1201/9781003241737

Typeset in Minion
by codeMantra

Contents

Preface

ALTHOUGH BORN LATE IN Nordic countries as a hit kids TV format, animation relies in this region on the heritage of the world's best children's literature, or children's TV too, if it were more known. Nordic Animation is now what the whole world wants in the postpandemic era. Its most successful brands tell about equality and ecology, and, on top of that, it has genderfluid characters who care for animals as much as those tiny and sad creatures—exactly how every child once in childhood feels oneself. Aren't we all anything but happy and funny?

Acknowledgments

Special thanks to Paul Hayes, Henry Scheinin and Jonathan Price for reading some early drafts, and Mari-Leena Kuosa for suggesting me to change the focus more international from the unfinished Finnish version of the book. Thanks for the support The Association of Finnish Nonfiction Writers gave in 2019 and 2020. And most of all, all producers, directors, animators etc., who make Nordic Animation.

Introduction

Greta Thunberg's face is not that of a happy child. When found demonstrating every Friday outside the Swedish parliament, she was angry at the world for neglecting the climate crisis. Thunberg was made world famous by adults who took her to their vessel and got her to speak in the USA and Canada (Figure 0.1).

FIGURE 0.1 Greta Thunberg attends a Fridays for Future strike on December 13, 2019, in Turin, Italy. (With permission from Stefano Guidi.)

DOI: 10.1201/9781003241737-1

1

In her speech held in the European Parliament in Strasbourg, France, on April 16, 2019, Greta said: "Around the year 2030 we will be in a position where we set off an irreversible chain reaction beyond human control, that will most likely lead to the end of our civilization as we know it. That is unless, in that time, permanent and unprecedented changes in all aspects of society have taken place. Including a reduction of CO_2 emissions by at least 50%."

When the pandemic hit the world, Greta was forgotten for some time, but we are still sharing her worries. What is most certain, when the Western world survives the worst recession ever caused by the pandemic and the war in Europe, there will be a climate change, which can mean the water world with the arctic areas melting, or the new ice age when the ocean waves change their way.

Biodiversity collapse is something that everyone who has grown up near the Arctic Circle and played in the woods discovering plants or spotting migratory birds or butterflies for your favorite spring pastime knows well. The arctic nature has been suffering the loss of species for the past 20 years, and it will vanish. We already know that for sure, and it makes our children sad.

Greta continues: "We are in the midst of the sixth mass extinction, and the extinction rate is up to ten thousand times faster than what is considered normal, with up to 200 species becoming extinct every single day. Erosion of fertile topsoil, deforestation of our great forests, toxic air pollution, loss of insects and wildlife, the acidification of our oceans—these are all disastrous trends being accelerated by a way of life that we, here in our financially-fortunate part of the world, see as our right to simply carry on."

Anyway, if Greta is sad and crying for help from the world leaders, in her neighboring country to the East lives the happiest people in the world. For the fifth year in a row, Finland has been ranked as the happiest country in the world, according to the *World Happiness Report* (https://worldhappiness.report/news/in-a-lamentable-year-finland-again-is-the-happiest-country-in-the-world/). Nordic countries Iceland and Denmark are also trailing behind Finland on the happiness index.

Nordics are Sweden, Denmark, Finland, Norway, and Iceland—five countries that seem to be pretty similar from a distance but do have their differences too. Scandinavia as a geographical term leaves Finland and Iceland out. Within that term, the unity stands more in the way the countries are located under one another's arms and holding together.

Then Scandinavian is used accidentally; I see no problem with including Finnish to Scandinavians, but there is something more in us—exactly like Iceland is the only Nordic country to have volcanoes and hot springs and Denmark has no mountains at all. Sweden is the biggest in population and for its geographical area. In history, it has ruled its neighbors, but it has been able to stay out of wars since the war with Russia (1808–1809) in which it lost Finland. Denmark might actually have a little bit of imperial history, too, although the more recent history from World War II left it under Nazi rule just like Norway.

Danes consider themselves the most liberal, although all five countries belong to the most liberal in the world. Young Norwegians did not necessarily feel so some decades ago, because there are stricter areas with religion ruling the society, just like in Northern Finland. A considerably big hop in accepting the differences has waved through all five countries.

Iceland has a population of around 366,000, and it has to be taken into consideration always with Nordic cooperation. For its small size, it has managed excellent from the perspective of global animation. Just like tiny Estonia, it could be considered an animation powerhouse. However, the case of Estonia is very different, as Estonia was part of the Soviet Union, and its outstanding animation studios were inherited from that era.

Iceland has always been an isolated island, but just like its banking sector once entered the global market, the animation studios with ambitious producers have managed to finance big-budget animated features. It still remains a slight secret how they did that, but I would like to leave a little mystery here with the fascination of Iceland's specific role.

North is the entity that defines the Nordics. It describes Norway and Finland the most. However, Sweden is the country that has the south too, that is close to Denmark with a liberal happy life; therefore, on the contrary, the North stands both for darker tones and sounds.

Nordic Noir is a fixed term used to describe the drama series with the police solving brutal crimes, especially murders. When the genre became very popular in the UK, the USA, and many other countries, there was a discussion about how Nordic Noir is reflected in animation. There are some examples of that; however, mostly Nordic animation is something different, and it could rather be developing into the next big wave in parallel to Nordic Noir or separate from it.

Nowadays animation is targeted at the whole family who are either viewing it on TV or going to the cinema together. Films for children are seldom that dark, although the Danish author Hans Christian Andersen is widely known for his dark or sad tales. Many of those have been animated, not only by Disney, who has the most known versions, but also by Danish television, and Danish film companies have versioned those. When Swedish and Norwegian talent is employed too, they are Nordic classics. In a similar way to Moomins or Astrid Lindgren's most famous stories, is it possible to define the genre of Nordic animation through them when the older adaptations have been made far away from their country of origin?

Rather than referring to Nordic Noir as a genre, the Nordic term should stand more for values in social politics. Therefore, the Nordic is associated with the following things:

- High level of free education with excellent and equal schools and universities

- Healthcare that is almost free; paid on taxes that are high but tolerated as a welfare system

- Equality between sexes, ages, races, etc.

- The use of technology and digitalization on a high level for establishing both equality and democracy
- Arts and creativity being part of societal life

Some of these things overlap in a specific Nordic way. For example, a high level of education includes art and design, from early education to professional studies. Furthermore, the design processes are used in public services; thus, design no longer refers to just furniture or cups and mugs. Finally, innovative learning capabilities follow holistic education where both nature and human rights are considered high.

Insurances in Nordic countries are taken for the sake of the worst possible catastrophe, not for the fundamental human rights that naturally come along with being born in a particular country. There is a saying in Finland that being born here is like winning the lottery.

For the first generation of digital nomads, where I have included myself, it has been also possible to leave and do your work from the tiny island in the Baltic Sea or from the sunny seaside bar in Vietnam. We had the choice to travel to most of the countries with the passport.

For the rest of the world, Nordics are seen as a culturally united region who are proud of taking good care of children's health, education, and even the programs they watch on TV. There has to be arts, "children deserve arts from a very early age," which has been the main motif for Annette Brejner, a founder of the Malmö Financing Forum of Kid's Content, the Swedish industry event recently renamed Mbrane.

We think that the world's best children's literature comes from Danish H.C. Andersen, Swedish Astrid Lindgren, Norwegian Thorbjørn Egner (1912–1990), and Finnish Tove Jansson, not to forget Icelandic sagas or Norse mythology, in general. In particular, Jansson's Moomins have inspired animators from Japan to Poland and Russia. If the most recent Finnish–UK co-production does not please the most devoted fans so committed to older versions, there will be always something left to tell. This is also the case when something totally different and new has been developed from Astrid Lindgren's and Thorbjørn Egner's classical books (Figure 0.2).

There are many countries in the world that would like to have the same socio-economic status as the Nordic welfare states. These include Baltics, who think the word "Baltics" refers to the war, while the Nordic refers to wellness, happiness, welfare, and strength. There are even specific terms for that, like Danish hygge or Swedish lagom, meaning always having a fair share. According to Brontë Aurell, it is part of Swedish cultural psyche, which is one of consensus and equality for all, being balanced with that (Aurell, 2017, p. 105). The word "hygge" on the other hand comes from Old Norse, and it means feeling satisfied. As it is used day-to-day in Danish, it does not refer to a physical description but rather a state of mind (Aurell, 2017, p. 106).

FIGURE 0.2 Swedish author Astrid Lindgren together with Finnish author Tove Jansson in Stockholm in 1958. (Karl Heinz Hernried , from the public domain.)

Sometimes it helps to look from the bit of outside, to see who we Nordics are and what is our special view of things. In 2017 and 2018, I was invited to BLON Animation & Video Games Festival in Klaipeda, Lithuania. It is a pretty coastal town that has a ferry connection to the Curonian spit, 98 kilometer long, thin, sand dune. The festival used to have well-organized joint events, not only to bath in the Baltic Sea early spring or have a communal sauna but also to have a chance of networking with Nordic and Baltic Sea animation and game professionals.

In 2018, the program featured animated films, game projects, and virtual reality applications. Particularly impressive was the immersive artwork by Vitalijus Žukas called *Trail of Angels*—a tribute to Lithuanian painter and composer M.K. Čiurlionis (1875–1911). The way Žukas invites to step inside M.K. Čiurlionis's symbolistic paintings (Figure 0.3) creates completely new kinds of realities. However, at the same time, it shows how a story begins. It is when the abstract forms turn into characters and living beings,

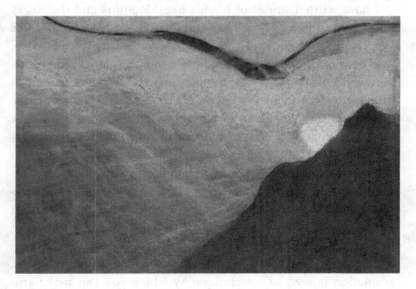

FIGURE 0.3 M.K. Čiurlionis, news, pastel on paper, 1904/1905, 64.2×90.7. (With permission of M.K. Čiurlionis National Museum of Art, Lithuania, Čt 216.)

and most importantly you start asking where do they come from, who are they, and what do they want from each other. Character animation is a very powerful form of art not only for kids but for adults too. This is the case, not only specially with Finnish–Swedish Moomins but also in some other creations that this book aims to present.

This book is about defining Nordic animation. Instead of looking back in the history, my attempt is to exercise the branding "Nordic animation" with the focus in those who have future prospects. The only history I can write about is for the past 20 years, which I have been involved with in Finnish and Nordic animation industry.

This book is Volume 1, and one day there will possibly be Volume 2 and Volume 3, written by somebody who is more eager to do historical findings or go deeper about some artists in the field. Writing about artists' work is a very sensitive area. I have tried to be as sensitive as ever.

I have written stories of brands like Moomins and the *Angry Birds*, studios like Anima Vitae and Qvisten, and individuals like Virpi Kettu from Finland and Veronica Wallenberg from Sweden, who have made their personal journey into the globalized animation world. Some stories are my personal eye-witness experiences from things that could also be told in another way. I could describe this also as a personal journey into the world of animation. If Tove Jansson's books have been comforting me in childhood, empowering throughout teen years and as an adult, LEGO systems have also been an important part of belonging to the bigger world.

I have sadly noticed that there are only a few books on animation. I look animation as an art form, although I am not an art historian, but a journalist who used to write about art. However, I might not be that deep like in Ivo Pikkolo's *Animasophy*, which is one of the best animation books I have read. In many books, animation is seen as a technique by which you can make animated films or a genre under children's television. Experienced in big trade shows, animation at worst is noisy and violent action for boys or childish and stupid lullaby illustration for the young-est audience. However, we can love *Teletubbies* as adults. We can appreciate animation as an art form, if art is important. For me, it is.

CHAPTER 1

Historical Findings

NORDIC ART SCENE REDEFINED

Painter Carl Larsson (1853–1919) is widely acknowledged as a synonym of the Swedish soul landscape. Her sensitive watercolor paintings portray family happiness and introduce the widely known term hygge probably for the first time—the interior design style with coziness that suited people of all ages, from very young children to grandparents (Figure 1.1).

FIGURE 1.1 Carl Larsson (1853–1919). (Courtesy of Stockholm City Museum.)

DOI: 10.1201/9781003241737-2

Larsson and her wife Karin had eight children together, although only six of them survived to adulthood. The whole family participated in decorating their house called Sundborn, later to become one of Sweden's main tourist attractions. Windows are small, but the garden surrounds the picturesque countryside living. There is some similarity with Claude Monet's (1840–1926) Giverny home. In Southern Europe, the period is known as belle époque.

In the north, it is precisely life within the family that appears as a paradise. Everyone takes their part in agricultural work. Horses, pigs, cats, and other farm animals belong to daily life. Lakes or rivers are nearby, and fishing is done as much as boating with kids. Harvest goes immediately to the big table. The family goes to the church on Sundays. Naturally, the church not only belongs to their life in the village but to the faith too—faith in good. Christmas highlights the perfection of the idyll.

The artist's studio is inside the house, and children are never perceived as outcasts from their artist father's work. Nudity is not a shame; women of the house and children pose for an artist with no clothes on. It is not a sexual thing, or it was, but we do not want to think about it. We want to see the beauty like the big flower buckets on the dining table and in the garden where family members have time to read or make handicrafts (Figures 1.2 and 1.3).

Larsson did not paint as expressively as his many contemporary impressionists. Instead, his lines stayed very visible, always beautifully drawn with a sensitive touch of a pen or a thin brush. And it may be that this fascination remains in the popularity of 2D animation in Swedish animation or Moomins, who appear as a parody for Larsson and his family, the Swedish idyll as its peak.

Denmark's first animator Robert Storm Petersen was a fan of Edvard Munch's paintings, who revealed the darker side of the more individual life. This individualism has been very important in modern art movements. Munch (1863-1944) was Norwegian

FIGURE 1.2   Carl Larsson Mamma's and the small girls room. (Courtesy of Nationalmuseum, Sweden.)

FIGURE 1.3   Carl Larsson: Breakfast under the Big Birch. (Courtesy of Nationalmuseum, Sweden.)

like the playwright Henrik Ibsen (1828–1906), who destroys the idyllic family life in the famous play *A Doll's House*.

Munch, being probably the most known Nordic painter of the modern era, slips into symbolism little by little. He takes influences from Japanese wood-cuts like other artists from the north, Vincent van Gogh, or German expressionists—exactly like the Lithuanian M.K. Čiurlionis.

Herbert Read writes: "…Northern tradition is in itself complex, but one fact is decisive—the classical acceptance of the organic world as a serene setting for human efforts, and art as a harmonious reflection of this world is not sufficiently expressive for it; it needs rather than uncanny pathos which attaches to the animation of inorganic" (Read, 1986, p. 53).

Read states that the tendency to abstraction reappears with redoubled intensity in the harsh times. He refers to the hostile and inhuman presence of nature, and it will be overpowered by fantasy: "Everything becomes weird and fantastic. Behind the visible appearance of a thing lurks its caricature, behind the lifelessness of a thing an uncanny, ghostly life, and so all actual things become grotesque" (Read, 1986, p. 54).

Although Munch visited Paris occasionally and stayed for more extended periods in Germany, Munch's isolation made him an outsider both geographically and psychologically. According to Read, his nearest parallels spiritually were Søren Kierkegaard and August Strindberg, Henrik Ibsen, and Friedrich Nietzsche.

Munch also expressed himself in poems that was typical to the expressionist artists. Furthermore, fantasies became the driving force in surrealist art.

Greta Knutson (1899–1983), a Swedish-born surrealist painter, was also a poet and an art critic. However, her art was overlooked for a long time as she married a much more famous artist Tristan Tzara. The other influential Swedish surrealist artist was Waldermar

Lorentzon (1899–1984), who belonged to Halmstadgruppen, the artists from the coastal city of Halmstad. The group also collectively made set designs for the Halmstad theater.

According to Sarane Alexandrian, *Manifeste du surréalisme* first inspired Swedish poets Artur Lundqvist (1906–1991), Gunnar Ekelöf (1907–1968), and Karl Vennberg (1910–1995). The anthology that contained their work was published in 1933.

In film art, Swedish filmmaker Viking Eggeling (1880–1925) did the abstract masterpiece *Diagonalsymfoni* in 1924. Eggeling was orchestrating color and forms with the time; the same way musicians handled tones and chords. It took him 3 years of total time to work with it. There was also a rolled painting with the same name done by a Swedish artist who was also a close friend of Tristan Tzara—one of the founders of Dadaism.

Danish equivalent of the Surrealist movement had a group exhibition in 1935 organized by painters Henry Carlsson, Elsa Thoresen, and Rita Kernn-Larsen, and the sculptor Heerup. While other Danish surrealists were rather abstract, Wilhelm Freddie (1909–1995), a giant surrealist figure in the country, was influenced by Salvador Dali's more realistic approach. His paintings were displayed in Copenhagen but banned from the London Surrealist exhibition in 1936. Those works have been called sex surreal for the sake of having sadomasochist interiors and overtly sensual objects.

Some art historians say that Tove Jansson (1914–2001)—the creator of Moomins—got familiar with surrealist art while living and studying illustration and technical drawings in Sweden. Perhaps, surrealist paintings lured her to create a fantasy world of her own, and maybe for her it was art equally to abstract paintings that were more appreciated in her home country , or a parody of the life of Finnish-Swedish rural burgeoisie. She did her first sketches from Moomins and started writing stories to survive the World War II terror. In Finland and Sweden, Moomins were known first as illustrated children's novels much before the animations.

POLITICAL CARTOONISTS PIONEERING
WITH EARLY ANIMATION

Looking back at the early pioneers of Nordic animation, there is only very little to be found in archives. For us, history opens mostly from other books with interpretations given by our predecessors in this job of making his-stories or her-stories. Many beginner films have disappeared, but some documentation has been done to prove who were the first ones in each Nordic country (Figure 1.4).

The majority of animation books are written in English for US dominance in the industry from Mickey Mouse to 1980s, when both Disney animation and the world animation dropped to give way to other audiovisual forms. In books that aim to cover the world animation, some chapters have been written about the French, German, or Soviet animation (since the early 1990s

Victor Bergdahl fyller en spruta . . .   . . . vars stråle magiskt målar ett porträtt.

FIGURE 1.4 A still image from the movie "Nar Kapten Grogg skulle portratteras" by Victor Bergdahl, 1917, featuring cartoon character Kapten Grogg and the author himself. (From the public domain.)

Russian animation), including the Estonians. Most writers skip Nordic animation like it had not existed at all.

Giannalberto Bendazzi (1946–2021) makes a nice exception in his book *Cartoons One Hundred Years of Cinema Animation*. The 1994 edition, which I found in the student library at Turku Arts Academy–Turku University of Applied Sciences, mentions Swedish Victor Bergdahl (1878–1939) and Danish Robert Storm Petersen (1882–1949) among the European individuals. "In many countries lacking structure and know-how, animation was left to the enthusiasm and extravagance of a few isolated amateurs, the so called 'pioneers'" writes Bendazzi, who was kindly assisting me with this book in May 2021 (Bendazzi, 2015, p. 16).

According to Bendazzi, there was a need for propaganda films; thus, animations served this often for satirical purpose. To my notion, the real aim for early animation to be commissioned by cinema owners was to entertain and first of all to persuade people to come to see movies in cinemas founded in city centers. When film was expensive, you have to create art with it and leave the business for educated artists—those who are making illustrations, painting portraits, and doing cartoons for newspapers, which in those days were political by their nature.

Victor Bergdahl was already an established artist and illustrator in Sweden, who had exhibitions and been to many magazines and newspapers of that time. Before devoting into arts, he spent 20 years on an old freight ship as a sailor, which is reported in his book *Till antibodies som beckbyxa* (1906). During this career, he made it all the way to Australia. Apparently, some unfortunate things happened to him during the journey. Thus, he decided to devote his time to his other hobby: illustrating, and he learned to do it with speed just like the animators are taught in contemporary animation schools from Singaporean Lasalle to Viborg's Animation Workshop.

The early pioneering animation art was not lacking quality, as it was done by artists. There was a lot to learn in techniques, and copying was one way to do it. In Swedish animation history

(Marko-Nord, Jurander, 2002, pp. 23–51), it is told that these young directors might have seen films by James Stuart Blackton or Emile Cohl (23), from whom they had possibly copied the use of living actors and animating postures (30).

It is often said that early animation is early experiments with the film format. Film practice before the industry with professional studios and the star system was nothing but experimenting in making moving images. Animation was one way to do it. The invention of a film camera made it possible to shoot the film, letting images to be joined to one another not as handicraft but with mechanical apparatus or digital in our times.

Leaving so much of the history out from this book, as I will skip some decades before the full bloom of the digital era, is an editorial choice. Been a child myself in the early 1970s, there was not so much to be proud of in the international perspective. And my generation was the first one really to reach out globally.

However, there are some early experiments that make an exception. There was a short period of making quality animation, but the best practices, such as cell animation, in general, were soon adopted for commercial uses, meaning that many artists' careers ended abruptly by a necessity of making money. After the period of wars in the first half of the 20th century, it could not have been affected more strongly in the development. This includes all the Nordic states.

Soviet animation raised high in quality in its cultural isolation, although the conditions for an individual artist were not that good. There was no concept of copyrights, but copying other's work or adopting the popular formulas had actually made some artistically interested works. 2D animation reached Disney in the 1950s, but interesting clay animation can be found too, such as the pirate Moomins made in the late 1970s.

Occasionally, short films are listed in books with great artists who created them, and I definitely believe that some Nordic animators from Norwegian hills to Finnish backwoods would deserve to be included there. They are just a few in numbers and shadowed by American or UK sisters and brothers. Liz Faber and

Helen Walters do exactly like that with their *Animation Unlimited Innovative Short Films Since 1940* (Faber, 2004), although they have something interesting to say about character animation. Faber and Walters have picked up Nina Shorina, who directed two episodes for Soviet clay Moomin animation. The first one of them was done by Aida Zyablikova, produced by the studio Souztelefilm. She told me that they were not paid to make animation, but they were supported while making animation (Vähäkylä, 2017).

Bendazzi lists both European artists who had tested the animation format in their experimental films but there are also many with the advertising background. The Italian-born historian notices how Swedish animation grew in the field of advertising but takes outsider Victor Bergdahl (1878–1939) into focus. Bergdahl animated comic strip characters in his 15 activist years. The most famous character was Captain Grogg, which also inspired Finnish comics arts of that time (Leinonen, 2014, p. 15, 19).

Captain Grogg is a sailor–fisherman–seafarer whose adventures remind me a little bit of Tintin and Captain Haddock. They go to exotic places where humor is met in surprising situations yet a bit sexist too, which might be forgiven as a curiosity. Swedish Bergdahl's career is considerably well recorded, and there is a good selection of archive material at Svensk Filmhuset in Stockholm, including film reviews from Filmbladet in 1917 (Linsen, pp. 347–349) and original drawings on cards for a full film. How fascinating!

Captain appeared for the first time in a short *Kapten Groggs underbar resa* made in 1916 and followed by 12 other shorts. Interestingly, they have been completely financed by one man— the director Charles Magnusson from Svenska Biografteatern— the local cinema owner. However, Berghdahl's first animated film is *Trolldrycken* in 1915 and followed by *Cirkus Fjollicnski* in 1916, which consists of 1,000 drawings that were made just in 6 weeks. Distribution was made possible by Svenska Biografteatern. Bergdahl could have had a bright future as an animator but there were wars to alter all ideals.

At all times, animation as a technique meets the conflict when thinking about the best available quality: Although it could achieve a wider audience, both locally and overseas, it has often been considered too expensive to make. Bergdahl's *Trolldrycken* was even exported to the USA.

Early animations had only 18 pictures per second (compared to 24 pictures). The export was done early from Sweden to other Scandinavian countries and Germany for films that were 3–5 minutes long.

Captain Grogg was originally named Josh Fibb, and it is actually a creation by Charles W. Kahles. As Bergdahl did not acquire any rights, and even the style and stories are similar (Marko-Nord & Jurander, 2002, p. 27), they just changed the name and continued working on the next film.

Kapten Grogg och andra konstiga kroppar, tenth in the series, had to wait half a year for its premiere. In the last film where captain gets fat, the bitter feelings become dominant in the character. Its creator felt it was time to get pensioned and turn into an advertising career, which was a way to make living for illustrators in all Nordic countries.

After Captain Grogg, which one could mark as the beginning of the character animation, Victor Bergdahl wanted to experiment Nordic cut-out and ignored the development with cell animation; therefore, his experiments remain short-lived. As an artist, he just got accustomed with one of the techniques. His last film was actually an animated documentary—an educational film about human reproduction *Sexualupplysningsfilm Från cell till människa*. It had only private screenings in Gårdlund hospital and never showed to the public in the cinemas. The film was commissioned by gynecologist Waldemar Gårdlund, and was meant to be used in his childbirth clinique and shows the fatal sequences through the development from fertilization to the birth of a child.

For its funny sometimes clumsy yet entertaining looks, many early animations suited well for educational content. It could have been a man drinking a bottle of alcohol and have delirium effects soon afterwards.

Bergdahl did totally 19 animated short films; 13 had Captain Grogg in them, making those one of the longest-lived European series in animated format, possibly shown in Russia and France too. According to Adam Marko-Nord, other films such as *Trolldrycken, Pelle Jöns,* and *Cirkus Fjollinski* increased the interest towards animated films around the country. Other illustrators were inspired by Bergdahl. And films were advertised too. In those days, short films could get almost equal space in advertising as the main picture. There could also be animation premieres on the following days. Swedish historians have found out that the day following Victor Bergdahl's *Cirkus Fjollinski* in Stockholm saw the premiere of Emil Åberg's film *Lille Calles Dream About Snowman* (*Lilla Kalles dröm om sin snögubbe,* 1916). Those were released in cooperation with Pathe, being the early activator of cinematic distribution.

Other films by Emil Åberg (1864–1940), who was also a painter, graphic artist, and illustrator, include *Mäster Tricks äventyr* (1916) and *Lilla fröken Synål* (1916). According to Adam Marko-Nord (2002), Åberg made seven animations in total in one year, which was in 1915 to be precise. In 1927, he traveled to Germany with many drawings, sketches, and letters telling about the trip where he had taken two films with him to be shown in local cinemas. Animation was born to travel, as has been heard many times by producers asking for finance from their local institutes.

Credit sequences for feature films could also include animation. In Sweden, those were made by Paul Myrén (1884–1951) and Arvid Olson (1886–1976) imitating the style of Swedish folklore. These sequences found in the most popular films of that time also made animation more acknowledged as a technique. Around 1920, even the election films for the Swedish social democratic party were made by using animation as a technique.

Historian Bendazzi finishes his short chapter from Sweden with painter Robert Högfeldt, whose 10-minute film *How We Tame a Troll* (1933) links with Nordic animation as an attempt to be defined in this book with the magical wood-dwelling creatures of Nordic fairy tales. Högfelt was born in the Netherlands, and educated in Düsseldorf and Stockholm. More known as a book illustrator in Sweden, *How We Tame a Troll* remained his only cinematographic work.

The film that changed everything in Nordic cinemas was Walt Disney's *Snow White and the Seven Dwarfs*. It started the import of American films. The popularity of locally made films sunk after American cartoons started appearing in your local bio, Kino, Joukola, or Nordia. Yes, until 2000 in Helsinki, there was a film theater with three screens showing Nordic films. Also, early film-makers have given up when the import took a hold both of the cinema offering and a common taste.

Hopping from Sweden to Denmark, Bendazzi spends most space for Robert Storm Petersen and links his work with the Danish newspaper comics that he had also created. For the early period from 1916 onwards, Storm Petersen also owned a tiny pro-duction company that released animated film. Animation was technically created by his operator and assistant Karl Wieghorst. *The Island* (1920) was the earliest known films, while *A Duck Story* from the same year remained unfinished. Many artists were reluctant to have their unfinished works shown in other Nordic countries. This is typical to the experimental phase of any art form. Without formal education and the tight guidance within animation courses, there are no teachers to decide when one's film is ready for the public screening.

A Duck Story, although, might resemble the characteristics of Nordic animation too with its subject matter, three men taking on for a duck-hunting expedition might also recall H.C. Andersen's influence. The other film that Bendazzi mentions from Storm Petersen includes *Rejuvenation: Professor Stejnack's Method*

(1921), but since the late 1920s he devoted more into the advertising career with some appearance in films as a comic actor. In 2008, A. Film produced *Journey to Saturn*—a film adaptation of Claus Deleuran's classic comic celebrating the 100 years since Storm P's first animated film. It was codirected by Thorbjørn Christoffersen and Craig Frank II.

Among the coeval competitors in the Danish animation field, Bendazzi lists Steve Brasch (1886–1970), a caricaturist and commercial artist whose work includes *A Rather Good Intention* (1919). Allan Johnsen is mentioned for his H.C. Andersen's film *The Tinderbox* (*Fyrtøjet* 1943–1946), which was saved from East Berlin just before it got occupied by the Soviet troops. The film opened in Copenhagen 1 year later and did not meet a good response among the contemporaries who had started to admire the Disney style as the only possible way of making animation.

If the early history of Nordic animation rather presents individual artists, Bendazzi has one studio from Denmark worth mentioning. That is Bent Barford's studio in the 1950s. According to Bendazzi, the best film of that era is *So Be it Enacted* (1964).

The reason why early Nordic animation can be seen as propaganda comes from the fact that early pioneers have been working as political cartoonists. This includes Eric Vasström, the first Finnish animator, and Tove Jansson. Both have been commissioned to do illustrations for *Garm* magazine (Figure 1.5).

In Finland, the first public screening of an animated film took place in 1914. Erik Wasström's (1887–1958) first animated short disappeared from his descendants' critical appreciation, but as a painter and a caricature artist his fame was known among Finnish scholars (Figure 1.6). *Garm* was a radical Finnish–Swedish magazine, which marks the beginning of the Tove Jansson's world-famous career, both with the Moomin character and opposing his father Victor Jansson's political ideals.

Both Tuula Leinonen, who wrote the history for Finnish animation for the centennial, and Heikki Jokinen, a Finnish

FIGURE 1.5 In-cover art for the *Garm* magazine Tove Jansson already used Moomintroll as a signature character. (With permission of ©Tove Jansson Estate. Photograph by the Author.)

journalist who has specialized in animation and comics, see Ola Fogelberg (1894–1952) the significant animator paralleled both with Bergdahl and Storm Petersen. His character Pekka Puupää, directly translated as Peter Woodhead, appeared in a 5-minute animated film and comics too but has a long continuity in live-action format with his bachelor partner Pätkä, which could be translated as Shortie. Pekka was married to Justiina, not the most pleasant wife while as she is seen constantly waving the rolling pin. After 13 hugely popular films, film director Pekka Lehto planned to make a gay version of Pekka and Pätkä and received development support from the Finnish Film Foundation for that, although the film remains unmade, which clearly shows both the mystery of the inseparable couples and their bubbling under-life from comics to cartoons.

FIGURE 1.6 The first Finnish animator Eric Vasström paints at Helsinki's Market Square. Photo by Finnish Heritage Agency, Pietinen collection. (Courtesy of Finnish Heritage Agency, Pietinen collection.)

Bendazzi also mentions two other animation artists from Finland: they are Yrjö Norta, whose film *A True Sunday Hunter* was released by Turku-based production company Lahyn Film, and Hjalmar Löfving (1896–1968), who was impressively productive to that era with 15 finished films, so that he could also be titled the grandfather of Finnish animation. Other names from Finnish animation picked by Bendazzi for his book include Holger Harrivirta (born 1915), Topi Lindqvist, and Eino Ruutsalo, who made quite impressive works with kinetic art. Ruutsalo's most famous works are engraved directly on stock.

There is also some printed research on Ruutsalo's art, which I leave out from my book though. Instead, I would dive next into Tove Jansson's (1914–2001) heritage on animated art. If my reader has a picture of Carl Larsson's Swedish idyll in mind, the Moomin family can easily be seen as caricatures of those. Although Tove wanted to be respected as a fine artist; however, her most important art is the creation of Moomin universe with many strange, gender-fluid characters radical to the bourgeois life of the era. Her paintings gave her income during the war years before the deal as a comic artist.

CHAPTER 2

Brands and Industry Beginners

MOOMIN ANIMATIONS – MADE IN JAPAN, POLAND AND THE UK

While H.C. Andersen's fairytales have been adopted by the Walt Disney Company, the Moomins were first animated in Japan, connecting them with the evolution of Japanese anime in addition to Nordic animation (Niskanen, 2010). The Finnish company Moomin Characters, founded in 1958 by both creators Tove Jansson and her brother Lars, sells licenses to make animated adaptations of the original stories found in both novels and comics.

If it takes a producer about 5–6 years to finance an ambitious project and requires roughly 20 years to see a return on investment, new versions do not come easy and without any conflicts. Nevertheless, among the animation industry, from the major players to small indies, many have had great interest in making versions of these popular yet unconventional characters.

Moomin comic strips were popular in the Commonwealth countries, but the Moomins were first known as illustrated children's novels in Finland and Sweden. The first theater play was made in Finland in late 1940s (Figure 2.1), and a decade later

DOI: 10.1201/9781003241737-3

FIGURE 2.1 Photograph of the premiere of the stage play *Mumintrollet och kometen (Mumintroll and the Comet)* by Tove Jansson, performed at Svenska Teatern in Helsinki in 1949. (Courtesy of Svenska litteratursällskapet i Finland.)

the first television adaptation—a puppet theater version—*Die Muminfamilie* was produced in the German city of Augsburg and directed by Harald Schäfer (1931–2001). The early series ran for two seasons, six episodes in each. The original puppets traveled to Helsinki in 2014, taking part in the Tove Jansson 100 years' anniversary exhibition, and were cherished by devoted Moomin fans.

Swedish Radio (then Sveriges Radio later SVT) honored Moomin's popularity by dedicating the very first children's program on Swedish television's Channel 2 in 1969. Tove Jansson wrote an original script for the half-an-hour show, not found in any books, and added the king as an extra character. This was followed by a Christmas advent calendar program in 1973. Half-animated and half-played by actors, *Mumindalen* was broadcasted in Finland 10 years later dubbed in Finnish. The actors played Moomins by wearing costumes, giving it an authentic 3D look. Voice acting was recorded afterwards. Due to the careful set design, the production could almost be regarded as animation, which it undoubtedly imitated. The director was Pi Lind and the producer Ulla Berglund—both employees of the STV's children's department (Edström, 2021) (Figure 2.2).

In 1980, Swedish animation director Johan Hagelbäck (born 1946) and his student Jaromir Wesely later in 1994 were able to animate two stories from the popular picture books *Vem ska trösta Knyttet* (in English *Who Will Comfort Toffle*) and *Hur gick*

FIGURE 2.2 Director Vivica Bandler (back row left) with her theater ensemble from Lilla Teatern and author Tove Jansson (first row right) visiting Swedish stages. Actors are Lasse Pöysti (behind Tove), Gunvor Sandkvist, Birgitta Ulfsson (in the center), Eva Perander, Jutta Zilliacus, Åke Lindman, and Börje Idman. (Courtesy of City Museum in Stockholm / unkown for Svenska Dagbladet.)

det sen (in English *The Book about Moomin, Mymble and Little My*) (Figure 2.3), because they were left out of the contract with the Japanese companies. The shorts, strictly loyal to the original book illustrations, were half-financed by SVT and half by the Swedish Film Institute along with the dynamic Swedish animation producer Lisbet Gabrielsson. Tove Jansson herself had her voice immortalized on the 11-minute film *Hur gick det sen*. Both films have been rerun on Swedish and Finnish TV and can be found in video compilations Bästa Knattefilmerna 2 and 3. A

FIGURE 2.3 Poster for the short movie adapted from Tove Jansson's first picture book, *The Book about Moomin, Mymble, and Little My* (*Hur gick det sen*, 1952) by Jaromir Wesely. (With permission of ©Moomin Characters™.)

DVD was released by the Finnish company Filmkompaniet in 2006 (Figure 2.3).

Outside the official licensed versions, there are Russian-language versions, one made in 3D clay animation and another version as a 2D cell animation; the former has a nice artistic quality, while the latter remains unrecognizable for character likeness. Only the stories that were then part of the Soviet curriculum were copied unmodified. However, the first Japanese productions already had the high talent to create animated worlds and movie characters, but they added many things from the Japanese society that did not match with the original Finnish–Swedish idealism. However, in the later stories, the fantastic and adventurous elements turned more psychological inner landscapers where the idyll became altered with non-idyll or discord (Holländer, 1983, p. 78).

Two early Japanese versions from 1969 to 1970 and 1971 had not been shown outside Japan until the Moomin museum in Tampere, Finland, received a few rare clips on loan for their exhibition in 2019. As a result of YouTube and other wild media platforms, many Moomin fans have also been able to view the pirate Russian-language versions and some episodes of the early Japanese Moomins (Table 2.1).

TABLE 2.1   The Japanese Moomins

The list below was created by the doctoral student Eija Niskanen to clarify the production companies and the directors of the first Japanese Moomin animations. It was requested by Finnanimation in 2010. Although Niskanen lived in Japan, she did not gain permission to view all the episodes for her study:

Moomin 1960–1970 and Shin Moomin 1972
Production companies: Zuio
Animation studios: Tokyo Movie Shinsha (episodes 1–26); Mushi Pro (episodes 27–65)
Broadcaster: Fuji TV
Producers: Masami Iwasaki, Yoshihiro Nosaki (episodes 1–26), and Masami Iwasaki (27–65); Predevelopment: Zuiyo Enterprise, Shigehito Takahashi
Directors: Masaaki Osumi (episodes 1–26) and Rintaro (episodes 27–65)
Key animator: Hayao Miyazaki (episode 23)
Animation directors: Yasuo Otsuka, Tsutomu Shibayama, Osamu Kobayashi (episodes 1–26); Hiromitsu Morita, Toyoo Ashida, and Mitsuo Ki-mura (episodes 27–65)

A very well-known 2D Moomin series with 78 episodes was made as a Finnish–Dutch–Japanese coproduction in Japan in 1990 and 1991. Finn Dennis Livson (1946–2013) was the producer, who had made contacts with the Japanese animation industry through his previous animated series *Alfred J. Kwak*. The success of the early 1990s series increased the licensing business for the characters, especially in Japan and Finland, and the first theme park was opened in Naantali, Finland, in 1993. For a generation of children and adults alike, this is the "real version." The hugely popular series was followed by a feature film *Comet in Moominland* (1992) directed by Hiroshi Saitô, and the film is considered a true anime classic as is the series.

The Polish version of the Moomins, originally *Opowiadania Muminków* (*The Moomins* in English), was made between 1977 and 1982, after the first Moomin animations were already rooted deep within the Japanese culture. The Polish version became very popular in England, where it was broadcasted on ITV, with the narrator Richard Murdoch, between 1983 and 1985, and was rerun in 1986.

The technical choice for animating in Poland in the late 1970s was different from 2D cell animation, which still resembled comics and book illustrations in Japanese versions. The Polish animators did stop-motion with soft materials like felt; therefore, they have also been called "Felt Moomins." The most sophisticated technique in use at the Oscar-winning Se-Ma-For studio was glass plates placed on top of one another to create a 3D effect.

According to Finnish producer Tom Carpelan, who acquired "The Moomin Originals" in the early 2000s from the Polish film archive, the best resources, talent, and materials were used in those days in socialist-ruled Poland and in combination with the most modern technology brought by the coproducer Jupiter-Film GmbH from Austria. The series was later reedited into a 78-epsiode HD series and sold to many new countries, including Brazil, while new animated features were also produced by Filmkompaniet (Table 2.2.).

Originally, all the materials for *The Moomins* were produced in collaboration with Tove Jansson and her brother Lars. Around the same time, Tove and her life partner Tuulikki Pietilä also made

TABLE 2.2   Moomin Features Based on "Polish Felt-Moomins"

The four Moomin features with their premiere year, based on original material made in Łódź, Poland.

- *Moomin and Midsummer Madness* (2008).
- *Moomin and the Comet Chase* (2010)—the first Nordic 3D movie. It featured talents like Björk (title song), Max von Sydow, Alexander Skarsgård, Mads Mikkelsen, Stellan Skarsgård, and Peter Stormare in the voice cast.
- *Moomins and the Winter Wonderland* (2017), featuring Stellan Skarsgård, Bill Skarsgård, and Alicia Vikander, coproduction with Animoon, Poland.
- *The Exploits of Moominpappa – Adventures of a Young Moomin* (2022), directed by Ira Carpelan, coproduction with Animoon, Poland.

the big Moomin House and many 3D scenes from different stories as a hobby. These form the base of the Moomin museum collection in Tampere, Finland. The Polish animation sets are displayed in the Se-Ma-For animation museum in Łódź.

The Finnish production company Handle Productions and the French company Pictak were commissioned by Tove Jansson's niece Sophia Jansson to make a film based on Tove Jansson's original black-and-white comic strips from the 1950s. This was an homage to Tove Jansson and to celebrate the 100th anniversary of her birth (Figure 2.4).

"In order to keep the feel of the film, the narrative, the dialogue, and the visual style as close to the original cartoons as possible, Ms. Jansson worked extremely closely with Xavier Picard and myself in developing the story, based on those strips. The dialogue in English, Swedish, and Finnish went through the same strict approval process," tells producer Hanna Hemilä.

Hemilä adds that the color scheme, criticized by some viewers for its old-fashioned tones, was inspired by the posters of the era, and the decision to use that palette was reinforced when they studied the color schemes Tove Jansson used in the early years of her painting career.

"No digital animation was used. 100% was hand drawn on paper. The papers were scanned and only thereafter was the process digitalized," explains the producer and adds that there are 50

FIGURE 2.4 *Moomins on the Riviera* press conference in Helsinki in September 2014. Director Xavier Picard (left), producer Hanna Hemilä (second from left), and Sophia Jansson (third from left). (Image provided by the author.)

boxes of drawings in all, taking up around 10 m³ to be found in Paris-based studio.

The artistic work for the film was led from France and Helsinki, Finland. "An exception was the hand drawing, which required a sizable studio. Since there were not enough available talented drawers in Finland or in France when the production was about to start, the hand drawing on paper was done in Suzhou, China," Hemilä says.

The anniversary film was sold to more than 70 countries, and it received positive feedback for its faithfulness to the original works of Tove Jansson. Among many fans, the floaty animation technique was not regarded as disturbing at all, although in the production year of 2014 the Finnish game industry was making enormous breakthroughs, and action was a keyword for the animation of the era. Some interactive Moomin apps have already been launched by a number of game companies in Finland, but their 3D style did not appeal to property owners.

In 2016, Gutsy Animations began developing *Moominvalley*—a brand new TV adaptation of Tove Jansson's much-loved Moomin books and comic strips. Gutsy Animations is an award-winning studio headquartered in Helsinki, Finland, and was founded in 2016 by Marika Makaroff, who also held the position of CEO until November 2020, before becoming Chief Creative Officer (Figure 2.5).

FIGURE 2.5 Marika Makaroff is the producer of *Moominvalley* series. (With permission of Gutsy Animations / Vertti Luoma.)

In Finland, Makaroff was known for an all-female talk show where politicians and businessmen were grilled by three gorgeous hostesses. Makaroff was the most devoted in the TV business, and she has worked as the country manager of Fremantle Finland and creative director of drama in Swedish Filmlance. At the time when she had to travel on ferries between Finland and Sweden, she came to the idea of making a new animated version of Moomins. When she approached me for the first time asking for advice on what kind of style she would make a new animated TV series, I recommended her 2D/3D, having no idea that it was our beloved heritage brand Moomins she was developing.

Since its early development phase, *Moominvalley*, with a budget of €21,100,000 for the initial 26 episodes, was set to become the most expensive Finnish television series to date. The initial concept art was developed at Piñata Animation and Illustration Studio in Helsinki, often regarded as offering the highest quality animation in Finland and working instead of its own IPs with the major industry players from Gutsy to Supercell.

Gutsy Animations then went on to set up an animation studio for *Moominvalley* in Bristol, UK, as a vast number of the series' crew was located there. The studio was also founded to allow the Academy Award and BAFTA Award-winning British director Steve Box (1967-), who acted as the series director for the show's first and second seasons, to participate in the production.

Developing a series based on such an internationally renowned and well-established IP as Moomin helped Gutsy Animations secure finances for this ambitious project. An Indiegogo crowdfunding campaign was also used to gather initial funds for developing the visual style of the series. International voice cast who joined the production, such as Rosamund Pike, Taron Egerton, and Kate Winslet, also provided great support in selling the series to international buyers and engaging Moomin fans around the world. Furthermore, English-language pop tunes featured in most of the episodes and the soundtrack albums from established and emerging artists are a significant part of the show's wider footprint.

However, there are people who don't like how contemporary pop music is accompanying the classic fantasy land, which could be located in any part of the world and in any time. Obviously, some Finnish fans would still like to hear Erna Tauro's songs made for the first Moomin plays. According to Virpi Immonen, from Kuumaa/Fullsteam Management, Makaroff is very familiar with both pop and classical music. The expertise in this field is being inherited from home. She also learnt in Sweden how the popular music can help new people to connect with the old brand, and exactly like the favorite drama series from HBO's *Six Feet Under* to Netflix's *Stranger Things* can raise new stars like Sia and classic favorites like Kate Bush with just one song. All music choices for *Moominvalley* season 1 are made by Marika and the director Steve Box, which also explains the English language. "English is the first language for the series, and the team has received good response from there," says Virpi Immonen.

Working with an iconic brand can be challenging in many ways. Fans come to expect a particular standard from that IP. From the beginning, Gutsy Animations was committed to upholding the highest quality in the Moomin projects and took significant effort to ensure Tove's work was respected when translating it for the screen. Gutsy Animations work in close partnership with the guardians of the brand at Moomin Characters.

According to Marion Edwards, Executive Producer and Managing Director of Gutsy Animations UK, four studios were asked to make animation tests for the series. Finnish Anima Vitae was selected as the animation studio, providing local expertise, and it enabled the production to apply for the Finnish Audiovisual Production Incentive readily when it was launched in 2017.

The first season of *Moominvalley* started airing in February 2019 on YLE—the Finnish Broadcasting company, and the second season followed a year later. The UK broadcaster Sky aired the first season in April 2019. In Japan, the first season launched on NHK BS4K in July 2019, closely followed by the second season launch in January 2020. In November 2021, the series also aired on a linear channel in Japan

(NHK ETV) for the first time, as the launch was delayed because of the Summer Olympics of 2021. The series has been sold to more than 60 countries around the world (situation: the end of 2021).

When production on the third season began, it was commissioned by the same anchor broadcasters—Sky in the UK and Finnish YLE, demonstrating the success of the series and its ability to resonate with audience. Some channels expect the Moomins or animation, in general, to be primarily targeted at small children. However, the Moomin brand and *Moominvalley* series stand for perfect viewing for the whole family to enjoy together a growing trend throughout the pandemic lockdowns. It was YLE Drama that bought the rights to the *Moominvalley* series, rather than the broadcaster's kids department, as it was able to provide greater investment in the series. This strategy enabled the exceptionally high budget for an animated show in Finland.

The COVID-19 pandemic and resulting lockdowns created challenges for the production of the international project. As the executive producer of the second season, Marion Edwards revealed that an array of locations were used by the crew and voice actors during recordings. For example, the voice director had to work remotely, as actors went to their local studios from Miami to Auckland.

Planning for season four of *Moominvalley* was under way in early 2022 and would bring many new stories to the show's vast international fan base. Furthermore, a Moomin-associated spin-off—*Woodies of Moominvalley* for a younger audience is also in development. At the time of writing, Gutsy Animations is also in negotiations with a major US broadcaster to acquire the *Moominvalley* series.

The popularity of Moomins as a design and literary brand has risen in the USA, partly due to the fascinating life of the creator Tove Jansson. In the past few years, Moomin fans from around the world have made YouTube videos exploring the history of how Tove Jansson created her Moomins. The rise in popularity of social media groups dedicated to the Moomins is more evident of the character's broad appeal.

FIGURE 2.6   Misabel character with Snorkmaiden. (With permission of ©Moomin Characters™ Gutsy Animations 2021.)

In the *Moominvalley* series, the cast was chosen with diversity at the forefront of the decision-making process; different cultures and races are represented to demonstrate the universality of the Moomin characters and the multiple genders outside the binary. Misabel's character appears at the end of season one in *Moominmamma's Maid*. In the original version, a trans-actor called Rebecca Root plays the role, while in the Finnish version the part is given to Miiko Toiviainen (Figure 2.6).

Toiviainen has appeared widely in the Finnish media and regards being a trans-man as something ordinary and a natural part of humanity. Toiviainen described the feelings involved: "Indeterminacy is easily associated with the Moomins. In their world, it is often needless to label gender or sexuality; the characters just are whatever they are."

In the summer of 2021, Gutsy Animations secured a €5 million investment from one of the most successful Finnish mobile gaming companies globally, Rovio Entertainment, creator of the *Angry Birds* franchise. Additionally, Rovio is developing and publishing Moomin IP-based games—*Moomin: Puzzle* and *Design* was soft launched by Rovio in December 2021 on Android and is

FIGURE 2.7   Original Swedish names for characters Thingumy and Bob as Tofslan and Vifslan (in Finnish Tiuhti and Viuhti), respectively, reveal the real persons they refer to: Tove herself and Vivica Bandler, who were lovers for a short time. Tiny creatures are hiding a big rubin in a big bag not to be stolen by Groke. The rubin can be interpreted as a symbol of love, heart, just like the characters together make the halves of the heart. (With permission of ©Moomin Characters™ Gutsy Animations 2021.)

inspired by the visuals of the *Moominvalley* series. In the game, players can decorate Moominvalley with blooming flowers, and explore the nature around them and make other explorations into the natural world. The game ties into the core values of the Moomin brand, including respect for nature, equality, friendship, and love (Figure 2.7).

DANISH ANIMATION BOOSTED BY LEGO, AND A FAMOUS WRITER

At least every second animation studio in Denmark has been doing something at some point for the LEGO enterprise. The company making famous bricks was born in Billund Denmark in 1932, and it is the world's most successful brand in licensing business (Figure 2.8).

FIGURE 2.8 *LEGO STAR WARS* figures pictured in November 2021. (From the public domain.)

The name LEGO comes from two Danish words "leg godt," which means play well. For its directors in three generations making quality toys has always been a key asset. LEGO has its biggest factory still in Denmark, which is also the home to the biggest LEGO theme park LEGOLAND® opened in 1968 attracts visitors from all over the world (Figure 2.9).

What is crucial to LEGO is how bricks stick together. Interestingly, this has also been a controversial topic in how strongly the brand can be present in CGI animations made by professional studios. "Stop-motion animations with LEGO bricks are mostly carried out by fans with no worries of legal matters. Often self-made animations go viral and become crazy successful," says Irene Sparre who worked as a line producer at A. Film and later took on the leading role while working with Wil Film on the biggest LEGO TV production handled by one single studio— 150 episodes of 22 minutes each. A total of 3,000 minutes of CG

FIGURE 2.9 Toy shop in Viborg, about 90 km north of Billund. (Image provided by the author.)

animation. With major networks such as Cartoon Network, Super RTL, and Disney and navigating rights owners such as Disney and Lucasfilm, these episodes were produced from 2011 to 2019.

According to Irene Sparre, Wil Film was initially a studio producing commercials, live-action shoots, and animation. It had not previously produced long format; the Ninjago adventures started with 4×11 minutes LEGO shorts and grew from there. The final breakthrough concept was a rare opportunity to produce *LEGO STAR WARS—The Freemaker Adventures*: The first standalone series under the *Star Wars* IP and the first time in history where a new set of characters is introduced outside the original *Star Wars* brand. This work put the company on the global map. LEGO's strategy was not only to use American scriptwriters and showrunners but also to produce "locally" in Denmark with cost efficiency and budget it wisely.

Irene Sparre says that a big turning point happened in 2013. LEGO's intentions at that time was to shut down the series. The plan was never to keep it running for years after years. But the fans revolted. They wanted more of Kai, Nya, Zane, Cole, Jay, and sensei Wu. LEGO listened to their fans and decided to venture into producing another six seasons of *Ninjago*. The biggest hype was taking place in 2014–2016. The internationally oriented toy company placed its creative decision-makers in Billund, Denmark. This meant a great deal for the Danish CG production team. "You could call them at LEGO directly on everyday production issues," Sparre says. "When long-format decision-making was moved from Billund to Los Angeles, you were competing with the clock. If you work until four in Denmark, it is just 7 o'clock in the morning in LA."

For LEGO working with US showrunners opened doors to the American market, and new collaborations with streaming services like Netflix and HBO were a natural next step. Today, LEGO Ninjago is running on Netflix, and *LEGO STAR WARS* is aired on Disney Plus. "Showrunners is a terminology originating from the US TV industry. We have the same deed for this particular function but not as much experienced talent to select from," Sparre argues.

For Danish producers, the concept was easy. LEGO brought the money and the distribution, and no investors were needed. The job was pure work for hire with little risk. To tap into the core DNA of LEGO, which means selling toys—approximately every fourth episode would introduce a new LEGO product for the audiences to purchase in the stores. "Making sure the CG representation of the brand and its authenticity was demanding and something difficult to achieve, as they are just blocks," Sparre admits.

LEGO identification elements have varied from one production to another and between the seasons. In *Ninjago*, it was not allowed to show the iconic LEGO studs, as this is for public broadcasters would be interpreted as a product placement. That is illegal in kids' content. "Leaving out the studs didn't mean we could not keep the iconic LEGO hands," Sparre says with a smile.

"On *LEGO STAR WARS* on the other hand, we could show the studs… as this IP was not LEGO's own," Sparre says.

Wil Film was never doing a LEGO TV series alone. Other studios important to LEGO include M2 in Århus outsourcing in Thailand and having India as its prime focus. Wil Film, on the other hand, has partnered with Chinese and Vietnamese studios, until it found a working relationship with Anima Point—the studio founded by Finnish wizards in Malaysia (Figure 2.10).

Sparre knew Jani Kuronen aka "Kurre" well from the Nordic TD Forum—an event organized by Sparre for 10 years (Figure 2.11). "We had met at Siggraph events in the USA and thought it would be a good thing to do something similar between Nordic fellows. Learning from one another was one of the key objectives."

FIGURE 2.10 Irene Sparre in the middle has been organizing Nordic TD Forum events. In 2018, it was organized in Hanasaari in Finland. (With permission from Sparre Productions/Mikkel Krgoh.)

FIGURE 2.11 Lecturer John Carey and Finnish Jani Kuronen from Anima Vitae at Nordic TD Forum in Hanasaari, Finland, in 2018. Photo by Mikkel Krogh. (With permission from Sparre Productions/Mikkel Krgoh.)

"Kurre's help was already needed in the production of *Ugly Duckling and Me!* (2006) at A. Film. I called him on Friday morning, and next Monday he came to Copenhagen," Sparre tells and continues: "It is more than a work relationship. It is about trust, the same trust we had with Qvisten Animation when we made [the] *Kurt Turns Evil* (2008) movie."

Director Michael Hegner has said (Hegner, 2012) that the vision with LEGO Ninjago was to create a simple yet appealing style around the LEGO minifigures. In the production, all unnecessary detail in the look had to be cut off and work with simple repeated elements, though reflecting the essence of LEGO. Outsourcing was important to keep the deadline and the budget. "Budget savings" were used on storyboard and animation.

"At the very start in 2009 we had a small creative team in Denmark to develop looks. It was CG artist Thomas Banner, 2D conceptual artist Bjarne Hansen, and me, and we were given the challenge to match quality and price. Outsourcing was necessary, but already within the first 2 years more than 40 people were working out of Denmark, increasing to 125 artists at its peak," the director counts.

Sparre tells that the Shenzhen-based GDC studio had a working pipeline for *Ninjago*, but there was no transparency in production. "They allocated their A team for *Ninjago*, whereas as *Ninjago* grew we felt that somewhat smaller *LEGO STAR WARS* production were somehow neglected. And we eventually decided on moving this production North. Sophie Animation in Dalian was responsible for five specials," Sparre explains referring to *Droid Tales* (2015) directed by Michael Hegner and Martin Skov.

Since starting her own company, projects have been written in Danish, and translating process takes many rounds. Sparre Productions have eight people in-house, one coordinator, and three directors. A couple of art directors are freelancing. The new series in development will most likely be on Netflix. Working again with an American studio on new assignments is also among Sparre's future plans.

Concerning Nordic coproductions, Sparre sees one major challenge, and that comes down to financing. Without having at least one of the bigger European territories, it is hard to raise the required funds.

Long before LEGO bricks, there was a man whose imagination has created charming fairytales inspiring both artists and composers alike. Hans Christian Andersen was born in Odense in 1805 and died in Copenhagen in 1875. His most famous stories—*The Ugly Duckling* and *The Little Mermaid* belong to the Disney Classics collection so closely that many fans hardly think about their Danish origin. Equally, the stories can be found in the Chinese curriculum, and books with the most popular tales can be found in Beijing bookstores where Tove Jansson's Moomins and Astrid Lindgren's Pippi Longstocking still remain an oddity (Figure 2.12).

FIGURE 2.12   Danish Hans Christian Andersen is considered the father of fairytales from China to South America. (Courtesy of National Museum Denmark.)

The Little Mermaid statue is a must-see for anyone visiting Copenhagen. In 2010, it was moved to Shanghai for the World Expo, a radical and also resentful gesture, but the Danish took it with respect. When Japanese artist Yayoi Kusama had an exhibition in Louisiana Museum of Modern Art in 2016, not far from the Danish capital, she illustrated and released the book on *The Little Mermaid* (Figure 2.13).

Anime version of *The Little Mermaid* dates back to 1975 directed by Tomoharu Katsumata Toei Animation as a production company.

The first Disney adaptation from H.C. Andersen tale was not *Little Mermaid* but *The Ugly Duckling*. Just an 8-minute short was released as early as in 1939. The Russian version from 2010 has Pyotr Ilyich Tchaikovsky's classical masterpiece *Swan Lake* as a soundtrack. It was made with a budget of only 1.5 million US dollars.

FIGURE 2.13 *The Little Mermaid* story has also been illustrated by Yayoi Kusama. (Image provided by the author.)

In 1998, Dansk Tegnefilm produced the animated story of the author himself. Marie Bro as a producer of *H.C. Andersen's The Long Shadow* (*H.C. Andersen og den skæve skygge*) was aimed at adults and directed by the veteran director Jannik Hastrup (b. 1941).

In his review of the biographical film for AWN, Finnish film critic Heikki Jokinen named Denmark "the little giant of feature animation," Jokinen thought that Denmark has produced several animated features through the years because of their good public support system to the cinema. He was impressed by how adult-targeted film expanded the format of animated features.

"H.C. Andersen's *The Long Shadow* is an intelligent story about the man behind the reputation of the well-known fairy tale writer. Ever since his early childhood, H.C. Andersen has had the feeling of being different, and he soon discovers he has a mean shadow that takes over from him. The shadow makes a fool of him, steals his loved one Jenny, and promises his soul to the devil. Throughout all of this, Andersen carries his pet duck along!" (Jokinen, 1999).

Producer Marie Bro explained to Jokinen that one-third of the 4.6 million Euro budget came from public support; the rest has to be made in Danish cinemas. H.C. Andersen's *The Long Shadow* got good reviews but only some 20,000 spectators. It was bought by several TV channels and was also distributed in French cinemas.

A. Film, the Danish animation powerhouse founded in 1988, made its modern version of the H.C. Andersen classic called *The Ugly Duckling and Me* in 2006. It was directed by Michael Hegner and Karsten Kiilerich. The protagonist of the film is a streetwise rat Ratso who finds an egg that hatches a mutant swan. Ratso soon starts showing Ugly as a freak. The script is cowritten by Hegner, Kiilerich, and Mark Hodkinson.

Jørgen Lerdam (Figure 2.14) has directed major Andersen stories for DR, Danish National Broadcasting Company. In total 30 episodes, aired between 2003 and 2005, and published on DVD as an English name, *The Fairytales* celebrated the 200th birthday of the fairytale father.

FIGURE 2.14 Maja Dich (left), who has worked for the Danish Film Institute also as a freelance producer, director Jørgen Lerdam (center), and Anders Mastrup (right) from A. Film in Mifa in 2017 when the Nordic animation booth was organized for the first time with joint forces. (Image provided by the author.)

Lerdam thinks that all H.C. Andersen stories are too sad and dark for contemporary kids. Sadness can also be a beautiful theme; the aesthetics of melancholy are common throughout Northern and Eastern Europe, reaching the possible peak in the story of *The Little Matchgirl*. It saw daylight as a Disney short as late as 2006, as the 1937 version was done by Columbia Pictures not Disney.

A. Film's CEO Anders Mastrup told me in Annecy in June 2022 about his background and favorites what probably the most important Nordic Animation studio has done. Mastrup was studying political history, but filmmaking was another option that he has never regretted since cofounding the studio with Kiilerich and four other partners after the successful *Valhalla* movie (1986).

Both Hugo movies, *The Jungle Creature: Hugo* (1993), directed by Stefan Fjeldmark and Flemming Quist Møller, and *Hugo: The*

Movie Star (1996), directed by Stefan Fjeldmark, Flemming Quist Møller, and Jørgen Lerdam, have been very important in the sense that the crew was making own IPs instead of learning from service work for big American companies. Denmark used to have a good comics scene. Many directors, including director Stefan Fjeldmark, came from that background and acquired their animation skills partly from afternoon classes taken primarily as a hobby rather than a profession. Fjeldmark has continued in animation and founded own companies in Denmark and Tenerife, Spain, after 19 years in A. Film.

Mastrup thinks that making *Help! I'm a Fish* (2000), directed by Stefan Fjeldmark and Greg Manwaring, and voice-directed by Michael Donovan and Michael Hegner, gave them international fame and brought *Asterix and the Vikings* (2006) to be made at A. Film. The French company in the film was M6 Films. Danish directors Stefan Fjeldmark and Jesper Møller got lots of respect and credit from this film with famous French characters. It was also a very important reference for Finnish Anima Vitae to choose A. Film as its main partner for *Niko and the Way to the Stars* (2008). Michael Hegner was more experienced as a feature director, while for Finnish Kari Juusonen it was his first feature length film. In a sequel to *Little Brother, Big Trouble: A Christmas Adventure* (2012), Kari Juusonen got much help from Jørgen Lerdam's experience in animation.

Olsen Gang Gets Polished (2010) was coproduced by Mastrup, Søren Fleng, and Tomas Radoor, directed by Jorgen Lourdes, and finally *The Incredible Story of the Giant Pear* (2017) and *Checkered Ninja* (2018) got coproduced with Trine Heidegaard.

With a background on TV business, producer Trine Heidegaard won already the Danish equivalent of the Oscars, Robert prisen from *The Trouble with Terkel* (*Terkel i knibe*, 2004) family film in 2005. In this teenage story, directed by Kresten Vestbjerg Andersen and Thorbjørn Christoffersen, Terkel's girlfriend commits suicide, and a maniac starts stalking him. Next feature with the same directors adding Philip Einstein Lipski to the team *Ronal the Barbarian* (2011) was nominated for Cristal in Annecy in 2012. Satirical fantasy film takes into the village of barbarians, and the main protagonist is nothing but a hero with no muscles and other barbarian traits. It has been seen as a parody of Sword and sorcery subgenre in fantasy literature as much as role-playing games and their association with heavy metal. The concept worked, I remember enjoying the film when it was shown at Cartoon Movie, a pitch forum, but in cinemas it did not become that big hit as expected.

The Incredible Story of the Giant Pear (2017), coproduced by Thomas Heinesen, had three Danish companies onboard: A. Film, Einstein Film, and Nordisk Film Production; however, for the next efforts Heidegaard founded her own studio Pop Up Production after 10 years at A. Film Production, then 5 years at Einstein Film, which she has also cofounded with Philip Einstein Lipski (Figure 2.15).

FIGURE 2.15 Producer Trine Heidegaard and director Philip Einstein Lipski are remembered from a funny pitch at Cartoon Movie 2017. Lipski made the audience laugh by presenting the low-budget hotel he was staying in that year. It tells about the reality of a Nordic animation director who often has to work as a freelancer and switch from one company to another after each project. (Image provided by the author.)

Since 1996, no Danish film has sold as much as *Checkered Ninja* (2018) "In the end, I thought it was time to be a 'woman in my own house,' so to speak, where I am a producer and also a line producer from time to time. My goal is to do really good projects, which is a matter of taste, of course. I always work with one project at a time so that everyone involved can focus completely on the task," Trine said in a 2021 interview with the Swedish *Monitor Magazine* (Dee, 2021, p. 40).

Checkered Ninja (2018), followed by the sequel *Checkered Ninja 2*, has been a great success in many countries, such as in France and Norway, but exceptional in Denmark. This action-packed teen film got 946,502 admissions in Danish film theaters by May 27, 2019. Over the last 30 years, no other film in Denmark has been able to reach the same level of admissions.

The "edgy" humor with a special tone and a visual language has not been liked by everyone. It was not received that well in Finland. Finnish critic for *Episodi* film magazine Niko Ikonen questioned in his review (Ikonen, 2019) if something is left behind the cultural barrier. The humor is too black and outrageous, the story even begins with a young Thai boy been murdered. "The spirit of the vengeful warrior takes over the bait of a ninja doll who swears death to all the capitalists who have spread injustice and deprive the child laborers of a poor country," Ikonen writes. For him, a bullying theme is also too much for the film he thinks is targeted at adults, rather than teens.

Checkered Ninja 2, on the other hand, was awarded with two statuettes in April 2022 at the Robert Awards for Best Children & Youth Film and Best Adapted Screenplay. The record-breaking *Checkered Ninja* was also an award winner in 2019 when it won three Robert statuettes, also for the Best Original Song. International awards for the feature includes BIAF prize given in Bucheon, South Korea, in October 2019.

Other powerful Danish industry personalities include Sarita Christensen (Figure 2.16) who got her first Robert from a live-action movie for children with many special effects. One year earlier she producer her first animated feture in Zentropa, famous for

FIGURE 2.16 Producer Sarita Christensen. (With permission of Copenhagen Bombay.)

obeying the dogma rules and its controversial lead figure—director Lars von Trier. Directed by famous cartoonist Anders Morgenthaler (b. 1972), *The Princess* (2006) gathered also nominations and awards from many film festivals.

The Princess tells a brutal story about a missionary August, who returns to a suburban neighborhood and is determined to take care of his niece 5-year-old Mia, who had been left to live in a brothel after her mother's death. Since child Mia is used to watching all sorts of porn. Initiated by her uncle, Mia and August destroy all the material in which "Princess" stars. The small child is dragged into the brother's revenge mission (Figure 2.17).

Technically the film is 80% animated and mixed with rough unprofessional video footage, which adds another reality level to the story and its central characters.

The festival round for *The Princess* that started at Cannes Film Festival took the film to numerous fantasy film festivals, where the complex subject was tolerated more than in children's programs. The box office remained minimal, and on television it was challenging to prevent children from watching the film with the extra cute protagonist. The references to anime style are mentioned in

FIGURE 2.17 *The Princess* is the half-animated half-VHS quality video footage mix made at the controversial production company Zentropa. (With permission of Zentropa.)

some reviews, and Mia looks a bit like the characters typical to Japanese artist Yoshitomo Nara.

Three years later *The Princess* premiered. Nara's drawings were used in the documentary *Platform*, which presents the sex trade in America. When he was lecturing in Finland in 2012, I heard from Nara that some festivals refused to show the film, as it was emotionally too hard; however, animated sequences soften the material to some degree.

After *The Princess* was finished at Zentropa, Christensen started her own production company called Copenhagen Bombay. Its main business idea is to focus and be as innovative in making children's films as Zentropa had been with adult films. The story is always of central importance; Christensen often works with different directors and scriptwriters and does not want to tell the same stories repeatedly, as often happens with animated features. "I would see it as a waste of taxpayer's money," says Christensen.

It is hard to break through internationally and raise the financing with something too original. However, Copenhagen Bombay is an exception, and its reputation echoes in Southern Europe and Latin America.

"Original does not have to be something weird. For example, our Halloween special for Disney Channel was very much inspired by [the] *Home Alone* movie. We just did it in our own way, and it developed into a different story," says Christensen.

Success in the international market is boosted with coproductions. Financing partners include Danish regional funds, Film I Väst in Sweden, and Nordisk Film & TV Fund, which started in Copenhagen but was later moved to Oslo, along with Danish and Swedish Film Institutes. Under Petri Kemppinen's rule it shown a lot of interest in the animated format.

The Great Bear (2011) takes two siblings into the midst of the mythical forest. When a gigantic bear kidnaps his little sister, 11-year-old Jonathan has to rescue her and overcome being a too cool elder brother. The style mixes 3D and digital cutout under the director of Esben Toft Jacobsen, to whom the film was the feature film debut.

The second film by Esben Toft Jacobsen, *Beyond Beyond* (2014), was produced by Swedish Petter Lindblad with a 2,500,000 Euro budget. It tells the story of a voyage by ship where a family of rabbits fights against sea monsters and other oceanic dangers whilst searching for the mysterious Feather king.

Coming to the streaming world era, Copenhagen Bombay has collaborated already with Netflix and HBO. After live-action, collaboration with Disney animated content is in discussion. Service work that we have done for Cartoon Network or Moonbug Entertainment in London has taught us a lot. Any project is training people to work faster, says Sarita Christensen.

Once you choose the hard genre, there have to be other ways to finance the extensive portfolio of 30 original productions. The content produced at Copenhagen Bombay has been sold to 98 countries.

Despite many tryouts internationally, Christensen has found it most cost-effective to stay in Denmark with the local talent and super superior pipeline. Outsourcing does not always count, as Denmark lacks some treaties in order to avoid double taxing. The company researched the Chinese market and used to have an office in Hong Kong. The ambitious CEO's mission is to grow the talent within the studio rather than looking for it elsewhere, which risks potentially the length of the production process and the delivery of the end product.

In addition to the production studio, the company has a sales department and an advertising agency. The future will show which divisions are needed in other parts of the industry chain.

In Cartoon Forum 2020, Sarita presented her new series project called *Høj*. It has been commissioned by DR to present Nordic gods to the new generation of kids aged 8–10. In the series, an oddly tall teenager dwarf called Høj runs away from home and goes on an epic adventure through many worlds to discover his identity. Values listed in the project presentation include accepting yourself, friendship, loyalty, facing challenges head on, learning from mistakes, and understanding the past. There will be dwarves, elves, giants, and many other creatures arising from the ashes, added with character transformations.

NORWEGIAN CURIOSITIES – FROM IVO CAPRINO TO HIS INHERITORS

The story of Norwegian animation follows a bit different path compared to Danish, Swedish, or Finnish. Although the country had some talented draftsmen like Svarr Halvorsen and Thoralf Klouman doing their experiments since 1913—the most important figure in 20th-century Norwegian animation is Ivo Caprino (1920–2001). Born to an Italian father, Mario, famous for selling handmade furniture around Norway, and a caricaturist mother, the granddaughter of the Romantic painter Hans Gude (1825–1903)—a master puppeteer who did some study trips to the Czech Republic and the UK but was practically self-taught, devoting all his life to making stop-motion adventures with funny and personal characters (Figure 2.18).

The fascination with his films stems partly from kind-hearted trolls found in Norwegian mythology and, in contrast, from high-speed race cars. The filmography of the early Norwegian master consists of three feature-length films, 38 commercials, and 16 commissioned movies. Altogether, Caprino's films have been translated into 14 languages.

Caprino's debut film was an 8-minute black-and-white short called *Tim og Toffe* (1949), but his international breakthrough, according to Gunnar Strøm, happened with *Veslefrikk med fela* (1952) when he won the children's film prize at Venice Film Festival in 1952. However, Caprino's most popular work is an 88-minute-long *Pinchcliffe Grand Prix* (*Flåklypa Grand Prix*, 1975) offering

FIGURE 2.18 Ivo Caprino and his mother Ingeborg Gude worked together until her death in 1963. (Courtesy of Billedbladet NÅ/The National Archives/Caprinofilm.)

comedic scenes with suspense and excitement. Both events and funny characters are animated by Caprino himself. While some earlier puppets were made by Caprino's mother, they were made by an apprentice in *Pinchcliffe Grand Prix*.

Two main characters of the film are Sunny (Solan) and Lambert (Ludvig) created by Kjell Aukrust in original novels. According to Caprino's son Remo Caprino, who made an EMMA-awarded video game based on the film in 2000, and worked as an assistant director and production manager for his father—they represent every human being's alter ego—the optimist and the pessimist. "That is one of the main reasons for the huge popularity of the film. This, of course, together with the charming story, the quality of my father's unique animations, as well as the elaborate work in every detail of the interiors and sceneries," the son describes.

The race car in the film is built and driven by cycle repairer Reodor Felgen, famous for a pedal-activated combined shaver and a raspberry picker. Now his ambition is to win a car race in order to defeat his former friend. Unfortunately, once an apprentice in Reodors shop has stolen plans and builds another car. The huge competition follows, but, finally, Reodor wins the race.

The voice of Reodor is played by famous Norwegian actor Frank Robert, who has also made many classical roles from Ibsen to Strindberg aside cabaret and revues. Other respective voices for the central characters are Kari Simonsen for Sunny and Toralv Maurstad for Lambert—equally famous Norwegian actors. The narrator, famous for being one of the best comedians in Norway, is Leif Juster.

Side characters in the film include oil sheik Ben Redik Fy Fasan, who pays Reodor in cash to support building a winning race car called Il Tempo Gigante. "The film was made before Norway became a rich oil nation," remarks Remo Caprino.

Caprino built a real car exactly like in the film for marketing purposes, and he was driving it during promotional events around the film's premiere in August 1975. Remo Caprino tells that the car has been kept by a family taking part in many shows, both in Norway and Denmark, where many fans come to see it.

Since 1975, more than 5.5 million cinema tickets have seen *Flåklypa Grand Prix* in Norwegian cinemas, which is a huge achievement in a country that has a population of about 4.5 million. The film is also shown on Norwegian TV on channel TV$_2$ every year on December 25 at primetime. Additionally, it has sold more than 2 million videos and DVDs in Norway alone. The game is still the most sold computer game in Norway.

Another country where the film is hugely popular is Denmark. "Quite a few Danes actually believe the film is a Danish production," Remo Caprino says.

The film has also been rerun on the Japanese and the Russian television, and Italian children of all ages love the film, whereas it is not that widely known in the UK or in the USA. In Finland neither the artist nor the film has been famous, and the fact has been checked with a few puppet enthusiasts older than my age. Instead, we were huge fans of the funny live-action *Chitty Chitty Bang Bang* (1968), in which a car is the main character. I also suggested the Norwegian classic having similarities with *Thunderbirds* (1965–1966) with fantasy planes and Lady Penelope's car manifesting an interest in classical cars, but Remo Caprino picks an even more interesting comparison, that is, George Lucas. "Quite a few critics claim that Mr. Lucas has drawn inspiration for the famous race in *Star Wars Episode 1—The Phantom Menace* from our race. It is said that the plot is too much alike to be a coincidence," Remo Caprino points out referring to a fan video found on YouTube showing exact timing with the commentator of Caprino's film and the events in the pod race sequence of Lucas's classic.

Some of Caprino's earlier films are based on folktales, which Peter Christen Asbjørnsen and Jørgen Moe collected by walking the mountainous country from South to North.

Ashlad, the Norwegian national hero, appears in films *The Ashlad and His Good Helpers* (*Askeladden og de gode hjelperne*, 1961) and *The Ashlad and the Hungry Troll* (*Gutten som kappåt med trollet*, 1967), where Ashlad meets the gnome in the woods and, in thanks for his kindness, is rewarded with the ship that can travel by land and sea, and air too. Helpers that Ashlad meets are equally helpful, but each in a completely different way.

Earlier shorts, a 15-minute *The Fox's Widow* (*Reveenka*, 1962) and a 12-minute *The Seventh Master of the House* (*Sjuende far i huset*, 1966) also base on Norwegian fairy tales collected by Peter C. Asbjørnsen and Jørgen Moe.

Karius og Baktus (1954) is told to be the favorite film by the Icelandic musician Björk. Two main characters of the short animation, Karius and Bactus, created by the Norwegian playwright and artist Thorbjørn Egner, are tiny tooth trolls that live inside the dentition of a boy named Jens. They lead a good life, especially when Jens eats white bread with syrup and later fails to brush his teeth. The funny yet educational film became Ivo's most famous short outside of Norway, causing a sensation at the Cannes Film Festival when the two central character puppets were stolen and again when Danny Kaye featured them on his television show (Simon, 2006).

The Danish fans have also been attached to the 13-minute film *The Steadfast Tin Soldier* (*Den standhaftige tinnsoldat*, 1955) from the popular story by Hans Christian Andersen. The film was a celebration of Andersen's 155th birthday. It has been shown worldwide from Argentina to Canada and even dubbed into Russian. Production companies include Dansk Kulturfilm and National Film Board of Canada (Figure 2.19).

The same year Caprino also made *Scampermouse in a Jam* (*Klatermus i Knipe*, 1955), which is based also on Thorbjørn Egner's script involving popular characters from *The Animals of Hakkebakke Forest*. *A Doll's Dream* (*Musikk på loftet*, 1950) was produced by Norsk Film A/S while many of Caprino's films were commissioned by NRK, Norwegian Broadcasting Corporation.

Televimsen, or Frank Telly in English, was a character, which was first hosting a talk show and later became the mascot for the company NRK. It was used for the first time in 1959 as a pause

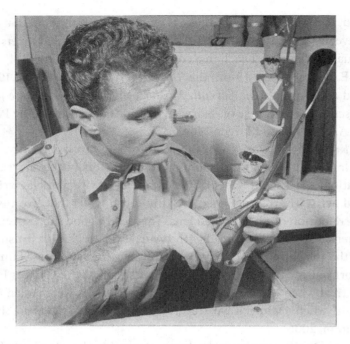

FIGURE 2.19 From the work on the puppet film *The Steadfast Tin Soldier* in Caprino's film studio in 1954. The main characters in this film were modeled by Ingse Gude. (Courtesy of Billedbladet NÅ/The National Archives/Caprinofilm.)

sign for technical problems on television. The mascot was animated by Ivo Caprino in 1961, and it appeared during 1962 and 1964 in many shorts. One could call it a TV comedian in an animated format. Being a puppet it could talk much more frankly than a human presenter when put to interview the most important people like the Norwegian prime minister. The episode made during Mr. Nikita Hrustsov's visit to Norway in 1964 did not avoid censorship by the head of the NRK.

With János Csak, the Romanian-born cinematographer, Caprino made the 17-minute documentary, which is a commercial for the city of Oslo. It mixes animated scenes taking place in outer space with aliens to the ancient Viking kings and queens.

Another important collaborator for Caprino includes Bjarne Sandemose, who brought many of his ideas into practice. He was an indispensable force in the studio and a genius when it came to technical solutions.

According to historian Gunnar Strøm, Caprino had a good sense of cinema, and his films are far from filmed puppet theater. Eyes were moving and brought character to dolls. In 1949, Caprino patented his klaviatur, a kind of mechanical keyboard, which made the work also economical. According to the son, he dropped his patent in 1954 and started using stop-motion (24 frames per second). "He felt this gave him much more artistic freedom," Remo Caprino says and has calculated that there are about 1.9 million movements made for the Pinchcliffe film only.

In a 1983 interview made by Giannalberto Bendazzi, Caprino defended his choice of realism with puppets and landscapes: "In my television programs, puppets discuss politics or current events. The abstract nature makes them interesting. If the same topics were discussed by actors, they wouldn't have the same meaning at all," Caprino said and added: "A feature film must have exceptional scriptwriting in order to succeed, in fact, we worked a lot on scriptwriting."

The son tells that Caprino never wanted to call his animated characters dolls; rather, they wanted to think that his work was to make them alive by giving them a soul.

Caprino's studio was located in Snaröya near Oslo, where many animators have worked from Trygve Rasmussen to the contemporary puppet artists of our times. Anita Killi has drawn inspiration from visiting the studio too.

Sentimental works by Norwegian Anita Killi (b. 1968) come close to those of Ivo Caprino, but they have transformed more to the 21st century appeal. With her moving stories and unique handcraft, Killi is mastering the art of making animation movies at her Studio Trollfilm situated in Dovre about 320 kilometres north from the capital Oslo.

Anita uses glass plates in her films, and combines this with puppets, skeletons, and a few digital effects. For example, materials like glitter and the air from breathing have been added digitally.

"My big inspiration has always been the animator Juri Norstein from Russia, since I first met him in Stockholm in 1989. From that day I have understood that I will work with this technique with cut-outs on glass plates," Killi explains her devotion to the Eastern European animation tradition.

Killi met the Russian animator while she was still a student at the art school in Oslo in 1989. She was captured by Norstein's animation style and the stories that were being told.

Killi herself studied illustration and graphic design at the Norwegian art school from 1988 to 1990, followed by studies in animation and documentary filmmaking at the Volda University College. The professor at the Volda University College Gunnar Strøm managed to establish a full-time animation study program in Volda by using the animation work that Anita had created. And, in 1992, Killi created her first 3-minute cut-out film called *The Glass Ball* with good help from her friend Hege Krogvik Bergstrand and Gunnar Strøm.

Killi then founded her own company Trollfilm AS in 1995 and finished her debut film *Daughter of the Sun* (*Lavrasiid Aigi*, 1996) a year later. The movie is based on a novel by Sami author Marry Ailonieida Somby. The 12-minute short movie is set at the Alta region by the Arctic ocean, where the midnight sun stays high throughout summer nights. In this landscape, a young Sami man has the ambition of capturing a wild reindeer by using his voice, but he gets lost.

The mystical film is accompanied by Sami music. Marry Somby's daughter Silja and Mikkel Gaup had the voices, and sang in both the Norwegian and Sami version of the film. The film won the Youth Jury Award in Algarve International Film Festival in 1997, and a year later it received the second place in the Chicago International Children's Film Festival. The film was again shown at the Wisconsin International Children's Film Festival in 2000.

The author Somby has been studying the life of Native Americans both in South and North America, and this has also been important inspirations for Anita Killi. She thinks that there are similarities between all indigenous people. "Lapps are our Indians. I learned about the nomadic lifestyles by setting up tents and making traditional shoes from leather, and wanted to become an Indian too," Killi recalls her idealist years and explains that she found inspiration Valkeapää.

Killi's movies, and her characters with beautiful big-eyed and sad-faced puppetry has gained fans all over the world. Her most successful short film *Angry Man* (*Sinna Mann*, 2009) (Figure 2.20) was awarded with the Grand Prix in Hiroshima International Animation festival in 2010. The movie received more prizes in 2010 than any other film, and this gave Anita Killi an Oscar Academy membership.

Hedge of Thorns (*Tornehekken*, 2001) has also won many international prizes. It tells a story of two children separated by the

FIGURE 2.20 From the short film *Angry Man* (*Sinna Mann*, 2009), based on Gro Dahle and Svein Nyhus' book about domestic violence. The film became the most awarded film in the world in 2010 and is Anita Killi's most important work. (With permission from Troll Film Anita Killi.)

war. In the beginning of the film they play on different sides of a creek symbolizing the unexpected dark happenings. The film has been a rerun in many festivals for its topic and screened in Belgium to celebrate Europe Day on May 9, 2022 more than 5,000 people watching it (Figure 2.21).

Death, war or a child's depression contra an adult alcoholism are serious issues but Killi thinks those can be handled in a poetic way. "Problems occur because you want to be happy and perfect. But the kind of films might be too dark for French or Latin American audience," Killi agonizes. According to her, Nordic societies are so safe that darker stories are accepted rather than in most countries. Even death should be discussed in a family movie She thinks.

Killi's 2020 short film *Mother Didn't Know* is a poetic fable telling a story of a young depressed girl who gets a little helper.

FIGURE 2.21 *The Hegde of Thorns* (Tornehekken, 2001) tells about the war breaking, and children are no longer allowed to play together, based on the book *Flon Flon et Musette* by Elzbieta. (With permission Troll Film Anita Killi.)

The background for the girl's depression, as the film suggests, is the girl's mother hiding her problematic drinking. I believe that there must be room for more serious and dark feature films, even for children: but you have to bring (the hope) in the end (Figure 2.22).

Killi says, *Mother Didn't Know* is Anita's first film that has been filmed digitally, while all the previous films have been made on 35 mm film. Killi mixes wooden bodies and cutouts that are made from wet paper with the special lighting: When the light shines through the characters, it makes a special effect. The wool that is used for the dolls comes from musk deer that live in the mountain area where Killi has set up her studio.

FIGURE 2.22 *Mother Didn't Know (Mor visste ingenting, 2020)* tells about depression among young people. This short is made as a promotion film for the feature film that Killi has been scriptwriting in 2022 called *Christmas Survivors* (Jula på Dovre). (With permission from Troll Film Anita Killi.)

The 17th century house where Killi's studio and her home are both, is restored to preserve the traditional lifestyle surrounded by huge valleys, older farms, and a beautiful alpine landscape. The landscape has been of great inspiration for Killi's feature film in development *Christmas Survivors*, which she was asked to do after the success of *Angry Man*. The feature got pitched at Cartoon Movie in 2014.

"There are far more animators today than 28 years ago when I started, and therefore there is also more competition over the same money," Killi worries. She would prefer to coproduce with other Nordics where common values and the legacy of Astrid Lindgren are shared. "In Nordics children are taken more seriously," Killi adds.

In Finland, the grand lady of stop-motion animation is Katariina Lillqvist (b. 1963) whose stories take also among other minorities like Roma people. Lillqvist started her career working inside Yle—the Finnish National Broadcaster. Until the late 1990s, Yle provided technical courses from recording sounds to editing film and video. Katariina passed her course to become an editor, but she was not keen on working with video as she loved holding film in her hands (Leinonen, 2014, p. 185). She finished a few documentaries before she got hooked up with animation and moved to the Czech Republic. There she learnt everything from local seniors specialized in puppetry. She has stayed most of her animator's time near Prague, where she set up her own studio and later an animation museum.

Lillqvist got worldwide recognition after her 15-minute short film *The Country Doctor* won Silver Bear in Berlin International Film Festival in 1996. Other Franz Kafka adaptations include *The Chamber Stork* (1994) and *Rider On The Bucket* (1992) for television, both 8-minute-long shorts. More recent world class shorts by Lillqvist include *Babybox* (2015), which was awarded for the best music in Annecy, and *Radio Dolores*, which is set during the Spanish Civil War. Lillqvist lended her personal family history to the story of Finnish factory workers helping the Spanish in the sinister war from 1930s.

In Finland, most attention from Lillqvist work has been gained by *The Butterfly from Ural* (2008), because its protagonist is a former Finnish President and a Commander-in-Chief in World War II. The film produced by Katariina's own company Camera Cagliostro, founded in 1992 and based in Tampere, has a questionable love affair between the war hero and his Kyrgyz servant. Tatu Pohjavirta, who has also practiced stop-motion along 2D animation, was assisting Lillqvist in the film making (Figure 2.23).

With *Mira Bala Kale Hin-Tales from the Endless Roads* (2001–2003), Lillqvist started transforming Roma tales into a

FIGURE 2.23 *The Butterfly* from Ural (Uralin perhonen 2008) is a short film by Katariina Lillqvist, in which the former Finnish President and a Commander-In-Chief in the World War II are suggested to have an affair with his Asian servant. (With permission of Camera Cagliostro.)

FIGURE 2.24 *The Last Matador* (2020) was made with the Praque-based team under the quarantines of COVID-19. Latex hands with all five fingers were borrowed from Polish Momakin studio. (With permission from Camera Cagliostro.)

stop-motion series for TV. It came out with six episodes. *The Last Matador* (2021) has another questionable hero: Vladimir Putin going bullfights to reflect his experiences as a bullied child (Figure 2.24).

CHAPTER 3

Studio Stories

MAKING IT ROUGH AND EDGY: HAPPY LIFE ANIMATION

One of Sweden's internationally most victorious episodes in animation was Happy Life Animation—a company founded in 1997 when animator and director Magnus Carlsson left Filmtecknarna and joined forces with commercial-minded producer Peter Gustafsson, also known as Piodor. Gustafsson is still continuing his career at Swedish commercial channel TV4 for scripted content, both for the Nordics and the Baltics.

Happy Life Animation entered the Swedish media landscape at the time of TV's commercialization. New channels were launched in Sweden, meaning TV3 and TV4. Cable TV also flourished internationally, and a hugely phenomenal MTV offered an arena for new visual storytelling. Despite various ways of financing crazy short animations, as a studio Happy Life was completely backed by Svensk Filmindustri—the major live-action film production company (Marko-Nord, 2002, pp. 48–49).

Torbjörn Jansson, once a creative director for the company but mostly credited for many scripts both for TV and cinema, says that the studio did not get bankrupt but was closed by its owners for not making

DOI: 10.1201/9781003241737-4

enough money in 2008. "It was spending a lot of money that came mostly from Germany, France, Hungary, and Canada," Jansson says.

According to the report made for Swedish Film Institute, Happy Life's production budgets were around 25,000,000–30,000,000 Swedish crowns per project. The economic base was made possible rather via commercials and music videos than by Swedish TV companies or the Swedish Film Institute. The Swedish financing remained 10%–20% (Marko-Nord, 2004, p. 12).

In the beginning, the company had nine employees, whereas the rest were freelancers. It grew up to 70 people at the time of the biggest tv show *The Three Friends and Jerry (De Tre Vännerna … och Jerry,* 1998–1999). This was created by Magnus Carlsson just like the *Robin* (1996, 1998–1999), which became a big hit on MTV, and its girlie follow-up *Lisa* (1998) ran on HBO Family and reached around 70 countries (Figure 3.1).

The international fame that Magnus Carlsson received for *Robin* was also noticed by the music industry. The Oxford-based cult band Radiohead asked Carlsson to make music videos using Robin as a character in those. *Rolling Stone Magazine* has listed the video for *Paranoid Android* as the 19th best music video ever made. *Rolling Stone Magazine* tells the story as such: "Thom Yorke

FIGURE 3.1 Swedish studio Happy Life Animations made international success with the series *Robin*. (With permission from Magnus Carlsson.)

was a big fan of Carlsson's twisted cartoon show Robin and wanted the video to feature the characters, but he didn't want it to include Gucci little piggies, androids, or anything else taken directly from the lyrics." Thus, he only passed the instrumental rendition to Carlsson and got a typically bizarre adventure between Robin and his buddy Benjamin, where they encounter a nude prostitute, bare-breasted mermaids, a sweaty, balding EU representative who hacks off his own limbs with an ax, and a man with a grotesque head protruding from his belly. "It is really about the violence around [Robin], which is exactly like the song," Yorke said. "Not the same specific violence as in the lyrics, but everything going on around him is deeply troubling and violent, but he's just drinking himself into oblivion. He's there, but he's not there. That's why it works." (Greene, 2011).

In addition to Radiohead videos, *Robin* appeared as the titular character on MTV's *Cartoon Sushi* series between 1998 and 1999. *The Three Friends and Jerry* aired on Fox Family until the channel was terminated by Disney in industry consolidation processes. The production had been outsourced to Eastern Europe; scripts, design, and project management were done in Sweden though (Marko-Nord, 2004).

Happy Life did mostly classical 2D animation and did not really get accustomed to the computer era. If Danish A. Film has also started as a 2D studio, it gets easily forgotten, as it has become known as one of the most efficient 3D studios in Europe. The same thing did not happen with Happy Life. When the company was closed by its owners, it not only meant the end of the cell animation era but also the rough style of Swedish animation.

Robin, as well as its sister production *Lisa* (Figure 3.2), has been seen as an imitation of *Beavis & Butt-Head* in its cult cartoon style. By some traditionalists, the style has also been called "limited animation" differing radically from the Disney style that is based on classic handicrafts. Only a few parts moved. The style

FIGURE 3.2   Magnus Carlsson's series *Lisa* aired on HBO Family. (With permission from Magnus Carlsson home archive.)

has its fans, but it has been also criticized for lowering the quality. Maybe it should be called a punk style in animation, if anybody for some time was able to become an animator with rough cut-outs from magazines, childish drawings, or clay animation. For some punk generation artists, e.g. in Finland Anssi Kasitonni made funny rough stop-motions in his barn and has gained a fan base with those. However, in animation the attitude "as a child of 6 can do it" is far from the truth, and no one should underestimate children these days, as has been noticed by Torbjörn Jansson with his own kids moving and playing and animating with programs they have downloaded on the internet and published on TikTok.

According to Jansson, in Happy Life, it was difficult to keep up with the edgy side, although it was applied in different genres and formats from music promos to an adult version of the Christmas calendar. If it worked making edgy adult or teen animation, Swedish directors wanted to make also edgy kids shows. However, there is a limited audience for it, and it is mostly the North American and European channels looking after it or maybe just Comedy Central.

Magnus Carlsson left Happy Life Animations in 2000 after directing three films about *Pettson & Findus*—one of the commercially most successful projects made at Happy Life and still running on German channels both in a series format and seasonally as movies. According to some statistics, 66% of 4–6-year-old German kids were watching the films with an old man and his cat as main characters in 2019, based on seven books written by Swedish Sven Nordqvist. In a story, a grumpy, old man lives with a cat that is not super cute or super clever, just a partner for the man who hardly deserves that.

Creepschool was a series project, which Torbjörn Jansson pitched in Cartoon Forum in 2000, when it took place in the Swedish town of Visby and was released after 4 years as a French–German–Swedish–Canadian coproduction. Running on German Kika, the series welcomed to the school where fears and nightmares nourished creepy reality. Elsa, Josh, and the other school kids solved their personal dilemmas and everyday problems, but in a twilight zone of *Creepschool*.

Pettson & Findus IV—Forget-Abilities (2009) was made at Studio Baestarts in Hungary and directed by Danish Jørgen Lerdam just like its predecessor *Pettson & Findus—Tomtemaskinen* (2005) produced by Danish Trine Heidegaard in A. Film and scripted by Swedish Torbjörn Jansson when settled in Berlin.

After running the Happy Life affiliate in Germany, Jansson started his own company The League of Good People (Figure 3.3), later Supresto Animated Intelligence having some funny animation projects in development though still waiting for a revival of classical animation with the growing demand of Nordic content. He thinks that in Malmö there could be a breeding ground for new animation start-ups, if the game sector were not paying animators and technical wizards that well.

The Finnish company belonging thinly to the post-MTV generation with excitable characters is Indie Films with Tomi Riionheimo,

FIGURE 3.3 Torbjorn Jansson has given up animation projects. *Micropunks* was a concept . His company The League of Good People was developing with Finnish Anima Vitae in 2010. (With permission of Torbjörn Jansson & Anima Vitae.)

who was a cartoonist before starting to sell bands' merchandise at rock clubs. *Rieku and Raiku* (1998) miniseries belongs to the era that started with Swedish *Robin* and was closed by the 3D dominance in animation until 2D tools were further developed.

Torbjörn Jansson told me about his trip to Finland in June 2001. He was supposed to meet with Tove Jansson and present her with some sketches that he has made about Moomins. Bull's Licensing in Sweden had told him that Telescreen license with Moomin Characters was close to its end, and they might be interested in making a new Moomin series. Unfortunately, Tove Jansson was in a coma, and Torbjörn only made it to Naantali, where he met with Dennis Livson—the producer for 1990–1991 Moomins animated in Japan. Later Torbjörn met niece Sophia in animation summer school in Jylland Denmark, but Sophia was not interested in the Miyasaki-influenced sketches on the Nordic property. At this time, Moomins had to be made as 3D characters familiar from games that the company tested.

Another Swedish talent from the classical era worth mentioning is Johan Hagelbäck, who has worked both on big brand TV series like

Alfie Atkins and shorts like *Who Will Comfort Toffle* (1980) based on Tove Jansson's picture book with the same name. *Hagelbäcks matrast* was a TV series where Hagalbäck is also acting as himself, starting every lunch hour by pouring sour milk on a tub, mixing it with different kind of ingredients, and eating it in the end of each episode.

ANIMA VITAE—3D VIRTUOSOS FROM FINLAND

If Denmark has A. Film Production, and Norway has Qvisten Animation, Finland has one leading 3D animation studio: It is Anima Vitae. It was founded in 2000 by Antti Haikala, Jani Kuronen, and Olli Rajala, all had been to the same multimedia course at Tampere University of Applied Arts still one of main schools educating animation professionals. In animation, there was only one course available for them in those days, and the teacher was specialized in traditional 2D. Lacking the tuition in 3D, they had to teach themselves. One competition win brought Antti and Olli 3D Maya license, and the rest is history. With

FIGURE 3.4 The Helsinki team for Finnish 3D studio Anima Vitae celebrating the premiere of Moominvalley series in January 2019. Antti Haikala in the center with Mikko Pitkänen on his right back and Olli Rajala on his right front are key personnel in the studio since the early 2000s. (With permission from Anima Vitae.)

Maya, the talented guys were able to develop the tools as well as the production pipeline (Figure 3.4).

As the first service work, the company started making computer-animated TV-series *The Autocrats* (*Itse valtiaat* 2001– 2008). It was a prime-time show for YLE produced by Olli Haikka's Filmiteollisuus and directed by Riina Hyytiä, reaching 233 episodes between 2001 and 2008. Hyytiä also directed the feature version *The Emperor's Secret* (*Keisarin salaisuus* 2006), which was the first Finnish computer-animated feature.

The Autocrats is a political satire, though its animated format also lured the smallest family members to follow it week after week. The characters are real-life politicians, some former and others to become future presidents. It is said that Sauli Niinistö, elected for his second term as Finland's 12th president in 2018, partially gained his popularity due to the series. He was skating on roller blades, and his sarcastic manners appealed especially to kids that have matured over time to be allowed to vote in the presidential election.

Another popular part of the satire was the final scene with two former presidents—Mauno Koivisto and Martti Ahtisaari, making their comments in the manner from *The Muppet Show*. *Spitting Image* is another program that could be mentioned as a reference to the Finnish CGI series.

With every new season, two or three new characters were added to give new ideas to a plot and keep it economically in balance. Scriptwriters included Atte Järvinen and Leo Viirret, both awarded with Finnish TV prizes Venla and Golden Venla. Expectations on the studio raised high too. Anima refined its pipeline into the mastery, and the story board technology used for the first time in the 85-minute feature *The Emperor's Secret*, both in speed and accuracy, giving it soon the title "the Pixar of Europe."

The production of *The Auto Crats* proved that "Anima" was probably the fastest 3D studio in the world in its ability to deliver material for Saturday night airtime, with the latest additions in the plot received at the studio on Friday morning. The series' slot after the main newscast and popular sports program did not have much chance to fail. However, when characters have only three fingers, their movements are a bit clumsy, and the coloring on their faces and hair started looking awkward with minor shading variations, the studio was eager to finish the series production at the beginning of 2008 to achieve other goals set by the studio founders.

As a fourth member of a founder team, Simo Savolainen is a graduate from the University of Jyväskylä in computer programming. He left the company in 2016 and has been coding games since then. The other key people in Anima Vitae include art director Mikko Pitkänen, who had worked in Anima mostly in full-time contracts since 2001, and Lasse Lunden, who was praised for the success in lighting. According to Pitkänen, who is a visual guy by his nature, all the four founding members are extremely talented both in technology and visuals, which has helped in making both successful features and series.

Anima has had influential females working in the studio, such as Sini Lindberg (Figure 3.5), who left for Germany to work at Pixomondo for same time. In 2020, Sini moved to Sweden, where she is working on Visual effects (VFX) productions. In Anima, she was a leading line producer for years. Laura Neuvonen was an efficient director both for *The Autocrat* episodes and two short films, which have been awarded many times.

Anima had once a strategy to build career for directors allowing them to make short films during the paid working hours; however, the selling point for two Niko films, in addition to the speedy pipeline, was the commercial for Finnair, the national airliner, where the realistic-looking hairy reindeer appears against the dark blue winter night with Northern Lights. Anima's success in the commercial side was also to animate pillar characters of the Helsinki central railway station for spots awarded in all major advertising competitions.

When Petteri Pasanen (b. 1965) was hired as a producer in Anima Vitae, his main task was to start internationalizing the company and creating intellectual property for them. Petteri had

FIGURE 3.5 Anima Vitae studio has visitors from Chinese TV station in 2014. Lua Zhou (Left) and Sini Lindberg (Right). Since leaving Finland Lindberg has worked for Trixter in Germany and Goodbye Kansas Studios in Stockholm, Sweden. (With permission from Anima Vitae.)

a background in live-action feature films. He had studied film production at London Film School between 1991 and 1993. He did his Masters in Economics at the University of Jyväskylä with a master's thesis on film marketing. Animation became his primary interest because of its international potential. While working with Claes Olsson's Kino Production, they made Katariina Lillqvist's puppet animations and funny videos for music duo M. A. Numminen and Pedro Hietanen.

Before joining Anima, Petteri's most significant success in animation was to produce Kari Juusonen's *Pizza Passionata*, the animated short that won the third prize in Cannes Film Festival in 2001. Juusonen was mostly self-taught in animation; he studied video and sound in Lahti, where his final assignment was an animated short.

Pasanen became the company's first CEO. His marketing excellence benefited the financing process for two Niko films, while the other Finnish producer Hannu Tuomainen created the great yet controversial story. *Niko Way to the Stars* (2008) held the top position as Finland's most successful film overseas (Figure 3.6), until the first *The Angry Birds Movie* (2016) was released. Niko's turnover exceeded most European and all Nordic animated features made by that time. Both films have Kari Juusonen onboard as a director (Table 3.1).

According to character designer Mikko Pitkänen, what is unique about the two Niko features takes place in the story. They tell about the broken family. In *Niko 1*, father has left both his wife and son to join Santa Claus's flying forces, a task admired by a young reindeer Niko more than anything. The son learns to fly on his dad's footsteps, and overcomes his fears and prejudices. Hannu Tuomainen and the other scriptwriter Marteinn Thorisson were awarded the Finnish Jussi prize for the script in 2009. The best

FIGURE 3.6 The first Niko film, called *The Flight Before Christmas* in the USA, was very succesful in France and Germany. (With permission from Hannu Tuomainen.)

TABLE 3.1 Box Office Data of Some Nordic Features

| | | | >10M USD in Box Office | | |
TOP 10	Title (English Name)	Year	Box Office	Budget (If Known)	Production Country
1.	The Angry Birds Movie 1	2016	$352.3 M	$73 M	FIN (CA)
2.	The Angry Birds Movie 2	2019	$148 M	$65 M	FIN (US)
3	Niko 2 Little Brother, Big trouble: A Christmas Adventure	2012	$24 M	€7.4 M	FIN (DK)
4	Asterix and the Vikings	2006	$22.5 M		FR (DK)
5	Niko 1 The Flight Before Christmas	2008	$22 M	€6.1 M	FIN (DK)
6	Little Bird's Big Adventure / Richard the Stork	2017	$14 M		NO (DE)
7	The Little Vampire 3D	2017	$14 M	€10 M	DK
8	Luis and the Aliens	2018	$12.6 M		DE (DK)
9	Solan og Ludvig—Jul i Flåklypa	2013	$12 M	NOK 25 M	NO
10	The Ugly Duckling and Me	2006	$11 M (IMDB) 580 K (int)		DK

Sources: IMDBPro, Wikipedia, Box Office Mojo.

Finnish film of 2008 was also Niko Way to the Stars voted by film industry colleagues and film critics alike.

The sequel from 2012 introduced Niko's little brother, adding not only cuteness to a family tale but also troubles as the film's title Niko 2—Little Brother, Big Trouble tells. The broken family gets new members, not only a stepfather but also a new younger brother (Figure 3.7).

Finnish name "Lentäjäveljekset" means pilot brothers, because flying exercises mean also adventure to these cuddly siblings. The film had a stereoscopic version, which was able to add some cashflow to the producers. If some critics have said that Niko 2 is

FIGURE 3.7 *Niko 2* or *Little Brother, Big Trouble: A Christmas Adventure* (2012) introduces new members for a broken family. (With permission from Anima Vitae.)

actually better than the first film, it was left without prizes if nominations are given profusely. However, many film competitions do not have enough categories, and for example art direction in animated films, or character design, if not layouts making unique universes are often more pivotal than directors' work. "Editing process of the animated features are made at the early phase and followed throughout the process, and needed to be in good hands with good in-house technology," says Antti Haikala, who edited and also coproduced *Niko 2*.

Anima Vitae was among the three Finnish animation production companies, which were part of the Finnish pavilion offering chosen by the Finnish Ministry of Trade for the Shanghai World Expo in 2010. The Pavillion's digital visuals were made in the studio. *The Daily Ape Show* running in the city taxis telling *Facts about Finland* was an exciting chapter. It had two ape characters as storytellers voice-acted by famous Finnish–Swedish standup artists Stan Saanila and André Wickström. The funniest episode tells about equality and Sweden. The love towards the neighboring country becomes apparent here. The Ape Show was later developed into a TV series that ran for 17 episodes on YLE, interested in keeping the rare adult animation slot in its place.

Since the Shanghai exhibition, Anima, among other Finnanimation network members, focused on the Asia strategy where China was a key focus with its exponential growth of TV stations and cinemas. The story how Anima Malaysia got started takes first to the Asia TV Forum, where Pasanen had traveled many times. For me, as a director for Finnanimation since 2009, it was the second time to visit Singapore in 2011. I found myself running after producer Yoki Chin—the Managing Director for Creative Media Point Sdn Bhd, as I had preliminary got interested in their character, DeeDee or Ddung, in those days (Figures 3.8 and 3.9). In Hong Kong FilmArt, I was told that the character design was made in

FIGURE 3.8 Ddung, later DeeDee, presented at Character and Licensing Fair in South Korea, that got the author interested in a particular company. This coincidence lead Anima Malaysia to be founded. (Image provided by the author.)

FIGURE 3.9 Malaysian Yoki Chin and Finnish Petteri Pasanen in Cannes 2012 celebrating their joint studio in Kuala Lumpur. (Image provided by the author.)

South Korea. I traveled there too to attend Seoul Promotion Plan—a joint event for Character & Licensing Fair. Koreans proved me, on the other hand, how Malaysians have made affordable animations, thanks to their support from MDEC—the agency that promotes digital industries in the country. The model had many similarities with the Singaporean scheme with MDA, but Malaysia attracted with its multicultural population more.

For Pasanen, the Malaysian studio was meant to be the gateway to the Chinese market, and he had ambitious plans to open the third studio in Mainland China soon after Anima Point, which was the name of the Malaysian studio for its first years. In practice, the running force for KL studio operationally has been the technical wizard Jani Kuronen. He moved there first and has been teaching 3D animation at the industry-ready school that Yoki Chin and his colleagues started with the government license. Luca Bruno, the talented, self-taught Finnish–Italian animator was soon following him. Nevertheless, Finnish employees have remained a few, as there is a diverse Asian talent pool to be exploited for many Finnish productions too.

Malaysian sister studio has proved to be a win-win success story through Malaysian tax credits and the Finnish Audiovisual Production Incentive launched in 2017. These incentives allowed other Finnish companies, like Rovio or Gutsy Animations, to benefit from Finnish talent in pipeline building and the cost-efficiency of animation production in Asia. Without the model, jobs in Helsinki could not be guaranteed in the competitive international market in the long run, and the success with new IPs will follow.

Although Pasanen left Anima Vitae in 2019, his primary interest lies still in developing quality animated features for the whole family. Anima Vitae got a new backbone from Aurora Studios, the company founded by Finnish business angels and run by Ari Tolppanen and Petri Kemppinen, the former CEO of Nordisk Film & TV Fond in 2021. New owner helps the studio to finish following features, such as *Fleak*—a creation by Antti Haikala about a young boy getting freed from a wheelchair into a fantasy world with a strange small creature, and *Niko 3 Beyond the Northern Lights*—the next movie following the reindeer family's adventures in Finnish Lapland. Both films have Nordic coproducers and directors. *Fleak* will be directed by Jens Møller, and *Niko 3* will be codirected by Kari Juusonen and Jørgen Lerdam. Producers in *Niko 3* are Antti Haikala, who has also created the idea for the feature, and Hannu Tuomainen, the producer in both the earlier films.

ICELAND: TWO STUDIOS AND 2,000 YEARS OF SAGAS

For its tiny size, Iceland has already been proved to be a miniature superpower for animation. Finding good partners is one of the key tasks for every animation production company, and Icelanders think about being a bit closer to America or as distant as Canary Islands from the mainland Europe.

Until recently young and talented Icelanders mostly moved to study overseas, but these days Reykjavík Academy of Digital Entertainment RADE has 2-year diploma studies in 3D technology, special effects, computer games, and animation. Icelandic financing sector had a period of overheated banking followed by the crash. In between, they could make good films and exceptionally good music.

Iceland launched its cash rebate as a first Nordic country in 2001, following Ireland, Italy, and Germany. Twenty-five percent tax reimbursement scheme is offered by the Icelandic Government on production costs spent in Iceland. It has succeeded in attracting some major American and European productions. Icelandic Film Centre has also dedicated coproducing funds for foreign projects that have elements of Icelandic culture. The grant can go to writing manuscripts, development, production, postproduction, and promotion.

Although there have been independent animators in Iceland, the first studio founded on its soil was Caoz in 2001. Its biggest effort so far has been to be the main producer of *Thor: Legend of the Magical Hammer* (2011) based on Norse mythology. The feature with more than 8,000,000 Euro budget with lots of private investing included was coproduced with Germany and Ireland as Ulysses Filmproduktion and Magma Film as coproducers. Magma's founder, the senior nomad, Ralph Christians used to live in Iceland, sharing big interest both in its magical nature and mythical past.

In a story young Thor, who is a blacksmith, lives happily with his single mother in a peaceful little village. However, the legend keeps disturbing the pleasant living, as Thor is believed to be the son of Odin, the King of the Gods. When fellow villagers believe that the terrifying Giants, who were believed to live in Finland in ancient times, will never attack them, but they are terribly mistaken. A Giant army crushes the village and takes the villagers to Hel—the Queen of the Underworld. Thor is knocked out and left behind. He sets out to save his friends with his magical weapon— the hammer Crusher.

Iceland's first feature-length CG animated movie succeeded well in South Korea, Türkiye, and Germany, among many other countries. It was shown at Beijing International Film Festival in April 2012 and sold to the Walmart supermarket chain in the USA. In Iceland, it won two Edda awards for the best set design and the best editor. The director was also nominated.

After the fortunate feature, Caoz's successes include a season for the TV series *Elias: Rescue Team Adventures* (2015) and a funny short film *Yes-People* (*Já-Fólkið*, 2020) nominated for an Oscar. The name comes from the only dialogue, "já" translated as "yes," used by inhabitants living in the same apartment block. The laconic film is directed by Gísli Darri Halldórsson, who has worked in many places and projects from Irish TV series *Olivia* to a feature *Two by Two: Overboard!* (2020), where usually paired Irish Moetion Films with Moe Honan and German Ulysses Filmproduktion with Emely Christians have found partners from Luxemburg for around 10 million Euro budget.

The second Icelandic studio GunHil was cofounded by Gunnar Karlssson and Hilmar Sigurðsson when they left Caoz in 2012. Gunnar did visuals and codirected *Thor: Legend of the Magical Hammer* with Óskar Jónasson and Toby Genkel. The name GunHil comes from their names. Hilmar Sigurðsson's also helms

FIGURE 3.10 *Icelandic GunHil* coproduced with Belgian Cyborn a feature, *Ploey—You Never Fly Alone* (2018). (With permission from GunHil/Cyborn.)

Sagafilm, Iceland oldest production company, making feature films, documentaries, TV series, and offering production services for TV commercials, TV programming, and postproduction (Figure 3.10).

CHAPTER 4

Beyond Games

Tech-Savvy Myths

THE CASE OF SWEDEN—FROM METROPIA TO NOSTALGIA

Metropia (2009) has been one of the most ambitious and unfortunate Nordic animated features. It was a coproduction with Film I Väst, which is a body that aims to promote film production in the area left behind by the car and the fridge industry. The film's financiers included SVT, meaning Swedish national television, Tordenfilm—an independent production company located in Oslo, and Zentropa Productions from Denmark. Money was also raised from Eurimages and Nordisk Film & TV Fond, along with Swedish, Danish, and Norwegian film institutes; EU's Media Program (later EU Creative Program); and local funds like Film Gävleborg. International TV channels contributing the production included YLE from Finland, NRK from Norway, and Canal+ from France.

The film is set in 2024, and all metro lines in the world are connected to one Metro. The film's visuals are gray, and all people are looking monotobored or desperate. However, nicely animated, almost with photographic look and feel, eyes having light in them

DOI: 10.1201/9781003241737-5

and the skin having wrinkles, it is raining through the entire film. Some people say that this feature project was the collapse of animation in Sweden. Big stars like Juliette Lewis or Udo Kier along with Swedish superstars from Stellan Skarsgård to Sofia Helin did not help much with the disappointment. According to the Lumiere database, it made only 15,949 admissions, the same year hits in animated feature genre included *Ice Age: The Meltdown*, *Up* by Pixar, and *Avatar*.

Producer of many Bamse films, Christian Ryltenius is one of those people who were working in *Metropia's* production and still active in the animation industry. He liked *Metropia*, and many of us wished for the better. It is not about clumsy characters walking odd way.

To my surprise, watching it again in 2022, it has not suffered with time. There might have been an idea to attract Japanese fans or the Black American audience for the Swedish film. Having experimental technique, the transitions from one world to another are just too big. In animation, if the illusion is broken, you easily give up following the story. When you do not like the character, you do not want to follow what happens to them. There can also be heroes and heroines in adult-orientated movies that we get attached to, but it did not happen with *Metropia*, and the Swedish Film Institute lost its interest in financing animated features. Only the most commercial ones succeeded, like Bamse films made in Malmö by Sluggerfilm, the company Christian Ryltenius found with Michael Ekblad in 2004.

There is a lot of realism in *Metropia*, but it would be better if it looked like drawn with charcoal.

Materially it looks a bit like a mix of plastic and old newspaper clips. Big heads have been torn from real world. Or, maybe, the main character looks a little bit like young Putin, so does Daniel Craig, and it never influenced the success of Bond films he played in. *Lilya 4-Ever* (2002) is a Swedish live-action film directed by Lukas Moodysson, and maybe these creators and their counselors wanted to create something similar in animation. It is a gray film on a gray subject, Russian Lilya to be trafficked as a sex worker to a Swedish town. She was looking after a better life but remains jailed in the most boring apartment houses. Her escape means motorway junctions with no return. Realistic yes, but in 2022 nobody wants to watch films like that. If they did in 2002, it does not matter if the format is animated, live-action, or a hybrid to any extent, it just does not work. In 2022, people rather want to escape to Carl Larsson's idyllic world with the family happiness, or to play as kids with the kids created by Astrid Lindgren in her children's novels, with the sense of eternal summer.

The sounds and voices in *Metropia* do not satisfy as; there is a kind of echo that makes you feel cold while watching the film. And it is often cold in film theaters. Voice actors don't talk; they rather mumble and stay fearful. There is a fear and emptiness in these characters when they take the suburban train and commute from home to work and from work back to home to heat the meal in the microwave and start watching telly. Ain't all animation meant to be funny one could say with some sarcasm?

Metropia works better in the small screen, you can say, and then there is a fan audience for it in 2022—possibly people who are fascinated about psycho things, who like talking about getting crazy, and who like the feeling of the moment when something in your mind is going wrong. There is a Penelope-looking woman, from the 1960s series *Thunderbirds*, and the tech-savvy person wants to be under her control. There is no hope than obeying and following the robots.

Some details have a fascination though. Stockholm underground entrance near Sergels Torg looks realistic, but mobile phones that had a funny slippery cover remind of Motorola world, the time before Nokia, and a long time before iPhones. They are all old looking just like in the 1960s sci-fi movies.

Street musician wears black glasses, old woman looks miserable, vertigo taking inside the eye, in the underground world where Metropia is set. Big-eyed characters do not look cute like in Japanese anime but scared. After watching *Metropia* for the first

30 minutes it feels like an hour. You get the feeling of been floating on the uneven surface. I like it, but I don't love it. In animation you have to make characters that you love, either there is a small child abused sexually or an old man living alone with a cat. People love silly, or angry, birds more than the alien-like characters of the Swedish postindustrial dystopia. Considering that Sweden has produced great live-action films, from a personified death speaking Swedish in Ingmar Bergman's masterpiece *The Seventh Seal* (1957) to painful yet realistic moments of *Lilya 4-Ever* (2002), it could have done better. And I do love both of these films.

Of course, there are Roy Andersson's films with laconic style, and Moodysson's earlier films *Together* (*Tillsammans,* 2000) and *Show Me Love* (*Fucking Åmål,* 1998) are both extremely funny; especially if you have been walking to school in the Nordic countryside. And the sugar in the bottom is the villain from Finland! *Border* (*Gräns,* 2018) is an excellent fantasy film about two trolls meeting in the customs and later on finding their sexuality together.

You cannot blame Astrid Lindgren, who is said to have hated Mickey Mouse all her lifetime, or the closing of Happy Life Animations, or Internet that we do not talk about Swedish animation in the same level as Danish, Finnish, or even Icelandic. I remember the time when Stockholm was considered the capital of new media; if there was an internet bubble, it blew up in Sweden bigger than anywhere, and possibly there was some ethos with the boom of digital animation, which still have not found Sweden. Or maybe in Sweden people just want things to be done differently; those Gladstone Ganders, as they are often called by the neighboring Finns, they know how to make profit or how to make the change in the world like a 16-year-old Thunberg taught us.

After founding Sluggerfilm, Christian Ryltenius and Michael Ekblad did not stop working and supervising in other studios both in Sweden and overseas. In Sluggerfilm, they had a different focus from Happy Life: "There was a need for new brands, but TV financing was not on a solid ground," says Ryltenius, who saw many pilots finished at Sweden's biggest animation studio. *Mamma Moo* (*Mamma Mu & Kråkan*, 2009) series was in making when suddenly TV stations stopped financing animation and computers were moved out from the Happy Life Animations studio. The episodes left had to be outsourced in Germany or Hungary, and only commercials remained done in-house, bringing some cashflow.

Financing new brands became impossible in the studio. However, Ryltenius thinks that very good animators and supervisors worked in Happy Life. Another "school" for a generation of animation professionals was Pennfilm—the oldest animation studio in Sweden that had its years of glory in the 1970s and 1980s. "It was too much under the shoulders of one man, Per Åhlin, who then stopped a few years ago, just retired. Pennfilm made only 2D hand-drawn animation, whereas Happy Life widened the concept to all formats and techniques," Ryltenius recalls more fruitful times.

In 1994, Ryltenius was animating the last season for *Alfie Atkins* (*Alfons Åberg, 1979–1994*) TV series in Pennfilm and directed nine episodes of *Björn Bear* (2004) in Happy Life Animations. Michael on the other hand directed TV series *ABC* for Pennfilm in Sweden aside many German productions.

"In Sweden, we are very nostalgic. We do not want to change things too much. Best children's movies and TV was made in the 1950s, and the good development lasted until the 1970s. Sweden is very conservative when it comes to children culture," Ryltenius explains.

While some broadcasters are conservative, in literature and comics more radical steps have been taken. "For SVT, The Swedish National Broadcaster, there is always too high risk to go to something extreme, and producers know this. They take no risks either, and this kind of animation does not sell overseas," Ryltenius mourns.

However, when the support from investors stopped, even big Swedish brands like *Karlsson on the Roof* (2002) was made in Oslo

Norway by Filmkameratene and *Pippi Longstocking* in Toronto by Nelvana. The big Canadian studio was not interested to make the Swedish golden jewel well enough, and too little money was spent in it. It could have been done better. But there are also other reasons; some people think that Astrid Lindgren's stories do not work on animation. Firstly, their characters are real children, instead of animals or some fantasy creatures. Thus, there is a reason to be nostalgic. Astrid Lindgren's live-action TV series are still the best children's TV outside animation. They are still extremely popular, and loved by any Swede from TV executives to financiers at Swedish Film Institute.

Metropia was a big challenge personally for Christian Ryltenius, who worked as an animation director in it for 2 years. "It is still unbelievable that it became made. Financing 350,000,000 Swedish krones, in total, was a miracle for such a dystopian film targeted at adults," says Ryltenius.

Ryltenius remembers the time when animation nomads were coming from all over the world to work in Trollhättan, in Western Sweden, where the work was done in the purpose-built studio in old industry conversion. The area has lost its heavy industries such as cars and trucks to growing Asian metropolis. Maybe, there was a bit dystopian feeling shadowing the area, and the mood of employees was reflected in the moods of film's recipients.

The film reception was a shock to its financiers and a director Tarik Saleh, who rejected animation after his debut. Although a prize for the best visuals came from Venice Film Festival, most reviews said that the film is too dark. "There was humor, but it did not come through," Ryltenius thinks.

Asking about why 3D animation has not develop into the same levels in Sweden as in Denmark and Finland, Ryltenius thinks that there is no reason to blame one film, which was rather experimental with real human faces and photographic looks. "All efforts have gone direct into video games. 3D in Sweden is gaming. There are good artists, but, most of all, money is there. Game companies do really well, and the interest in film is weaker."

Trollhättan had a 3D school for some time; it was more like a college, and students were doing 3D. In Gothenburg, it is possible to study postproduction, but students end up in VFX firms. Animation education remains in lower level than the university level; it is given in smaller places, in the middle of nowhere, places like Åmål, where the most creative students cannot live. Ryltenius and Ekblad studied both in Canada, in Sheridan College, whilst no animation courses were available in Sweden. A small municipal Eksjö had the first university-level animation school, but it operated under Konstfack, which is a famous art and design college founded in 1844. Both Tove Jansson and her partner Tuulikki Pietilä have taken courses in graphics and illustration there. Sweden is also lacking an influential animation festival like Fredrikstad in Norway or Animatricks and TAFF in Finland, or Viborg and VOID - International Animation Film Festival in Copenhagen Denmark.

After his studies, Christian Ryltenius worked as an animator in *Space Jam* (1996) in the USA, in *Captain Bluebear* (*Käpt'n Blaubär—Der Film,* 1999) in Germany, and in an Italian–German coproduction *Momo* (2001) based on the wonderful novel by Michael Ende, to name a few examples from the period. Michael Ekblad is also an VFX artist.

"There is a problem in keeping the employers," Ryltenius says. "Hiring them is easy, but to offer full-time work is harder. They will move to other firms. Thus the industry is lacking continuity."

Three *Bamse* films that Ryltenius has been producing are a mix of comic and animation. The brand is very commercial but also part of Swedish culture, kind of Swedish Mickey Mouse that everyone knows. In Sluggerfilm, they wanted to give films a more modern look than the 1970s comics, and it works. Bamse has its loyal fanbase.

"All films have done well in Finland and Sweden. Norway is ok and the Baltic countries too, but German or a French premiere, that the films had, were not that successful. Films have also been sold to Russia, and the fourth film is on its way," Christian lists.

Pelle Svanslös (2020) was hit by the pandemic, and no comparable stats are yet available. However, the second feature on the nostalgic brand is in planning. "It can possibly go well into streaming services," Ryltenius thinks referring to hopes with new VOD platforms such as Viaplay.

If the Swedish soft money is hard to get for animations, there has been problems with Nordisk Film & TV fond too. "They do not put any money into sequels. They are only supporting original ideas. That is a rule which should be changed. Distributors agree with that they want to be safe," Ryltenius says. Reading some reports made in Sweden it was said that the idea of making Nordic animation came from inside Nordisk Film & TV fond, and the Swedish have been the most reluctant to lose a bit of their national identity that comes to its great success in TV drama, mostly in its darkest formats (Table 4.1).

TABLE 4.1 TOP Swedish Animated Features

		Box Office	Budget		
Pettson and Findus (Pettson & Findus—Katten och gubbens år)	1999	$8.3 M		Happy Life Animation	SE (DE)
Bamse and the Thief City	2014	$4.2 M	€2.6 M	Tre Vänner Produktion AB (Sluggerfilm)	SE
Pettson och Findus—Kattonauten	2000	$2.8 MM		Happy Life Animation	SE
That Boy Emil (Emil & Ida I Lönneberga)	2013	$1.9 MM	SEK 28 M €3 M	Filmlance International	SE
Peter-No-Tail (Peter Svanslös)	2020	$970,000		Sluggerfilm	SE
Desmond & The Swamp Barbarian Trap (stop-motion)	2006	$500,000	SEK 4 M	The Jolly Patron (Assorted Nuts)	SE
Bamse and the Witch's Daughter	2016	$431,000		Sluggerfilm	SE
Beyond Beyond	2014	$226,595	€2.5 M	Copenhagen Bombay	SE (DK)
Metropia	2009	$81,000	€3.7 M (SEK32 MM)	Atmo Media Network/ Film i Väst (Sluggerfilm)	SE (NO)
Bamse and the Thunderbell	2018	$4,900		Film i Väst/Sluggerfilm	SE

Source: ImdbPro.

NOT ALL BIRDS ARE ANGRY—
ROVIO AND ITS SUCCESSORS

Rovio—a renowned Finnish company behind the Angry Birds universe—was born a gaming company. Rovio and its offspring are yet to solidify their place as a world-scale entertainment company after 4.5 billion game downloads and highly interesting brand extensions. In animation, the company's biggest achievements so far have been two of the successful features ever made from a video game property—*The Angry Birds Movie* (2016) and *The Angry Birds Movie 2* (2019) (See the Table 3.1 and Figure 4.1.)

For some time, the game giant had the biggest animation studio in Northern Europe in Espoo Finland. The studio made multiple series of 2D shorts and launched Toons TV—a multiplatform channel for showing series such as *Angry Birds Toons* (2013–2018), *Angry Birds Stella* (2014–2016), and *Piggy Tales* (2014–2018), along with some international titles like South Korean *Pucca* or *Canimals*. The studio was Mikael Hed's dream come true, which wasn't always met with enthusiasm from other stakeholders in the company. Hed was the CEO of the company from 2009 to 2014.

FIGURE 4.1 *The Angry Birds Movie* (2016) is by admissions the biggest Nordic feature ever made, grossing more than 300 million US dollars in cinemas worldwide. It is also the most successful film made from a mobile game. (With permission from Rovio Entertainment.)

The Rovio success story began in 2009 when Rovio's game number 51 took the Finnish game company from rags to riches. Everyone in Finland knows the story as such: Rovio, which means bonfire, almost went bankrupt before the success. *Angry Birds* was a simple game with a simple idea that worked. Above all, it was launched at the right time. For the people who were not constantly playing video games, the *Angry Birds* became their first and only game they downloaded on their new iPhones and soon on iPads—devices with perfect dimensions for a game where birds and pigs fought against each other.

Rovio hired people like Mikko Pöllä to help add more depth to the somewhat superficial game characters by building backstories for them. Pöllä worked with Mikael Hed daily for one hour via internet calls scripting the first *Angry Birds Movie* with the Los Angeles-based producer John Cohen. Writer Jon Vitti joined the project later. Sessions taught both Pöllä and Hed a lot. "Many character personalities had been inside Hed's head, but it required teamwork to transmit their behavior into a good plot," says Pöllä.

The first movie was a huge success, grossing more than 350,000,000 US dollars compared to any other European or Nordic animated feature. Only Aardman's *Chicken Run* (2000) had grossed 225,000,000 US dollars and was ranked between the two AB movies with their commercial success. French movies compete mostly with other French language movies.

Mikael Hed explains that there were many misconceptions about how the first movie influenced Rovio's revenue. The game department was more robust and more independent than the animation department. The animation unit was keen to collaborate with other units, while the game developing teams felt this to be less important due to their overwhelming position as the leading source of money brought into the company. From the outside, it seems the games eventually won the battle with Rovio for not having again focused its efforts mostly on gaming in the past few years.

Mikko Pöllä says that each division inside Rovio had different audiences in their minds, and each unit wanted to drive the

FIGURE 4.2 Hatchlings were introduced in the first *The Angry Birds Movie*. They learn to become angry with their enemies but also being cute to attract younger audience to play games. (With permission from Rovio Entertainment.)

brand too. "Licensing dep was making baby clothes, animation dep headed their toons to preschoolers, while games should have been directed to adults," says Pöllä (Figure 4.2).

The movie that brought the cute Hatchlings to the arena could be interpreted as a desire to lure kids to play games. Another way to interpret the adding of the newborn young birds coming in different pastel colors and soft feathers would be the company's interest in Japanese market in the second half of the 2010s. Company has already been doing well in China.

It is a well-known fact that the kids gaming sector does not create as much income as games directed to those already sporting their own credit cards. The Moomin games struggled from the beginning, as the grannies seldom play with their grandchildren. Among the Nordic game industry, the champions like Supercell in Finland or Swedish King had a working revenue model with in-game advertising and microtransactions. The average player for Supercell's *Clash of Clans* spends 50 Euros a day, but there are many who spend thousands a day.

Rovio has made some excellent cross media campaigns with the world-scale players. My personal favorite was a project where Finnish president Martti Ahtisaari (1994–2000), who negotiated the peace in Namibia and was awarded a Nobel Peace prize in 2008, is asked to do the same between the game's big enemies—birds and pigs. Clever brand extensions included cook books and theme parks, who were so well marketed in China that their Finnish manufacturer almost drowned under the over-flooding demand. Then an interest in consumer products business collapsed for a while. One could say the brand was overexploited.

Rovio's animation studio grew in 2012 from just 20 people to more than 100 employees. Rovio acquired animation studio Kombo in that year, but that was far from being the main reason the growth spurt happened. Kombo, the small studio, where character designer Lauri Konttori and line producer Nick Dorra were working, had made *Ella and Alex: A Suprise Birthday Party* feature in 2011. Based on the cute 2D design by Joonas Utti and Eliza Jäppinen, the short music video versions of the IP had found some fans, but the young theatrical audience in Finland did not adopt its sing-along concept. The film made only approximately 43,000 USD at the box office, but limited to Finnish cinemas that is very little for a film directed to a whole family (Figure 4.3).

The speed at which the Rovio studio grew had its downsides. It has been said in 2014 by Steve Pegram that the studio with over 100 employees couldn't even make the short format series by themselves, and those, like the girlie series *Angry Birds Stella*, got outsourced first to Anima Vitae's studio in Malaysia and second to Cube Creative Computer Company in France. "It was wrongly restructured," Pegram retains. Most employees were recent graduates from the arts school. However, the atmosphere in the studio was extremely creative. Visiting the studio in 2012 or talking to some animation nomads moving to Finland late 2013 from overseas, you had to pinch yourself that you are actually in Finland (Figure 4.4).

FIGURE 4.3 Nick Dorra pitched a new series at Cartoon Forum with his own company Haruworks Ltd. in 2016. The property also bases on the game. (Image provided by the author.)

Angry Birds Blues (2017)—a series about Jake, Jay, and Jim, the bluebird triplets as well as *Piggy Tales* were outsourced to Ferly—the company started by Mikael Hed, Laura Nevanlinna, Joonas Rissanen, and Ulla Junell-Pulkkinen in Helsinki and Vancouver. Originally called Kaiken Entertainment, the original idea of the company was to develop new IPs into bigger brands through 360° concepts and to work with third party IP in helping them to grow their business in animation, licensing, and publishing. This has been done successfully with properties like the Sweden-based *Star Stable* and Ferly's own project *Momolu & Friends*.

One of Ferly's cofounders Ulla Junell-Pulkkinen says that it was essential to be close to the market and its decision-makers. Ferly, having its base both in Europe and Canada, had the possibility to put together the financing for a new series like *Momolu & Friends*, a 78×7-minute preschool series.

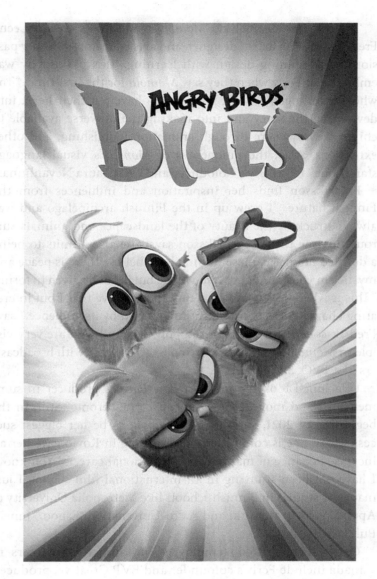

FIGURE 4.4 *Angry Birds Blues* was produced by Ferly, the company founded by Mikael Hed and other former Rovio employees. (With permission from Rovio Entertainment.)

The original idea behind *Momolu* world by its creator Leena Fredriksson—an artist, designer, and arts educator—was her passion for combining design with learning. This philosophy was embraced at Ferly when they saw *Momolu* for the first time: "The whole team together with Fredriksson have put their heart into developing the story and into making the universe available to children everywhere through animation, publishing, and other extensions. Also, the uniqueness of *Momolu*'s visual language stands out," tells Ferly's Cofounder and CEO Laura Nevanlinna.

Fredriksson finds her inspiration and influences from the Finnish nature. "I grew up in the Finnish archipelago and was always struck by the beauty of the landscapes and animals surrounding me there," Fredriksson says. She also admits to being a devoted fan of Japanese minimal aesthetics. There is peace and mysticism you cannot put into words, but it can be given in forms. "This is where my creativity stems and the love that I put in creating characters that are meant to be loved by its audience," says Fredriksson. The influence from both east and west are very visible in *Momolu & Friends*, starting to air in 2022 with broadcasters like TVO, SRC, and ITV.

Ulla Junell took the job as a *Paw Patrol*'s producer in summer 2020 and moved from Vancouver to Toronto. Still, in the beginning of 2021, she thought *Momolu* to be her biggest success so far. She is committed that working in Rovio gave her an increased chance of making an international career. "You know, I have not been studying in an international film school. I just made my studies in Finnish schools like Metropolia University of Applied Arts in Helsinki and Aalto-University in Espoo," Junell-Pulkkinen lists.

Other former Rovio employees building their careers in Canada include Ferly's cofounder and EVP Creative, producer, Joonas Rissanen and the director, Meruan Salim. Meruan's talent has been recognized at many Canadian studios, from Bardel Entertainment, to Disney, and to Sony Imageworks. He was the main director for the 2D episode in *The Angry Birds*

Movie—the most expensive animation minutes done inside the Nordics.

In Europe and Canada, several production companies have continued developing and producing Rovio's short format series, which have become immensely successful in both YouTube and Netflix. A long form series, *Angry Birds Summer Madness* by UK–Dutch-based Cake Entertainment was launched on Netflix in January 2022. Tom van Waveren told about the process of developing it with a mixed group of writers—a team based in the USA—having a showrunner and a script runner like in a typical American model: "First window is Netflix, which has a license, but it can be sold to other channels," Tom van Waveren says.

Van Waveren has lived in Copenhagen for some time. He sees both similarities and differences between Nordic countries. "The Danish film subsidy system is very good with advance payments. Finnish have done better with limited resources. In smaller territories, budgets are smaller too, and it is hard to make them commercially successful. People love Angry Birds characters, and the company also had a working model that was taken direct to consumers with box office returns," Tom van Waveren says.

The comet-like success with the Angry Birds brand reflected in European animation for a short while. This was remarked by some moderators in Cartoon events, both Forum and Movie, around Europe, although it has to be said that every bird character has its own birth story and universes, where bird lives differ from one another.

One could think that specially in Finland, some brands tried to succeed taking tiny steps after Rovio. Where the *Angry Birds* have their own fantasy island, Islandic *Ploye* reflects the Nordic nature along with *Niko* films and *Pikkuli's Starlight Reindeer*—a feature in preproduction in 2021.

Seeing a bird, specially a dove, as a symbol of peace goes back to the Bible or Pablo Picasso, who used a dove in his lithograph for the Paris Peace congress's poster in 1949. Flocks of birds in Nordic countries have a strong meaning related to the change of seasons. Every fall migratory birds leave, and they come back in spring. Nordic people spot from each species how close the summer is. Most spectacular birds flying in V formation are Eurasian cranes, but Icelanders think that Golden Plover is a bird that brings summer.

According to director Gunnar Karlsson, the first day of summer is always celebrated in April in Iceland, because it is mostly the light that makes summer in a country that seldom is reached by heatwaves. Gunnar is a codirector for *Ploey—You Never Fly Alone* (2018). The other director Árni Ólafur Ásgeirsson passed away in 2021 at the age of 49. The story is written by Friðrik Erlingsson, and it revolves around a plover chick, who has not learned to fly when his family migrates in the fall. Thus, the poor chick must survive the arctic winter, where vicious enemies threaten him to be reunited with his beloved one's next spring (Figure 4.5).

At Cartoon Movie in Lyon in March 2015, Gunnar and Hilmar pitched the next project called *Red Waters*. It is based on an opera by Lady and Bird (Bardi Johannsson & Keren Ann Zeidel). Also a sequel for *Ploye* is in making and presented at Cartoon Movie in 2022. In *Ploey 2*, the world is threatened with an endless winter. A young idealistic plover and two unlikely feathered heroes; a street-smart snake charmer and a legendary warrior who is past his prime, set out on a perilous thousand miles journey to foil the plans of the evil Ice Queen and her fearsome army by signaling the arrival of spring in order to fulfil an ancient legend.

Norwegian Kristine Knudsen produced *Richard the Stork*, also known as *Little Bird's Big Adventure* in 2017 with her German company Knudsen Pictures in Berlin and coproduced with her Norwegian company Den Siste Skilling in Bergen. Other coproducers are Mélusine Productions from Luxemburg, Ulysses Filmproduktion from Hamburg, Germany, and Walking the Dog from Belgium. Knudsen's connections with Germany came through her film production studies at Filmakademie Baden-Wurttemberg in Germany. In 2018, she won the Bavarian Film Award for The Best German Children's Film.

FIGURE 4.5 *Icelandic–Belgian Ploey—You Never Fly Alone* (2018) has been a big hit in many countries, telling about a bird who is left by his family migrating in the South. (With permission from GunHIl/Cyborn.)

The adventure follows storks, who foster an orphaned baby sparrow, which they think is one of them. When it is time for the birds to migrate to Africa, it is revealed to the sparrow that he is a different bird that is supposed to stay on the ground. However, he decides to prove himself that he can survive on his own. Allying with a pygmy owl named Olga and a parakeet named Kiki residence birds make their travel on ships, buses, and trains to find

FIGURE 4.6 *Pikkuli* series was broadcasted first time on Finnish YLE in 2015. The episodes also travel in many festivals. (With permission from Sunineye Productions.)

Richard's missing family and rescue his stork brother from a honey badger. The sequel was in making at the time of writing this book.

In Finland, there is quite a persistent brand *Pikkuli*, named Lil Birdie for some time. It is created by Metsämarja and Antti Aittokoski in Turku Finland. The series had YLE as a broadcasting partner for the first season. It is committed to the second too, but other financiers are still missing (Figure 4.6).

Individual *Pikkuli* episodes have been selected to numerous festivals around the world where they keep finding new fans thanking creators for dealing with many difficult topics and emotional skills. The series was nominated for the Pulcinella Award—the Best Preschool TV Series in 2016. Metsämarja was also asked to pitch the series in a competition in Hangzhou China, and she won it. At the time the Chinese coproduction was supposed to start, the pandemic put things on hold. The production has also employed students from Turku Arts Academy.

Another Finnish property considered by some journalists to have the potential to become the next Angry Birds phenomena in Finland and worldwide was *Dibidogs* series. The series with dog characters remind *Paw Patrol*, launched 4 years later than *Dibigogs*, rather than *The Angry Birds*. Been developed by two Finnish market research professionals, both new to animation but deeply in love with it, they created the series by making use of Finnish creativity lessons and holistic education. Some characters, events, and even the name for a place where dogs live ("Bonecity") were created at children's creativity workshops organized in Asia (Figure 4.7).

FIGURE 4.7 *Dibidogs* characters have many similarities with Paw Patrol. Finnish–Chinese coproduction was for a while the most watched TV series in Thailand. In Finland, it was aired on commercial MTV channel. (With permission from Futurecode/BlueArc.)

Solatie used contacts from his Chinese teacher to get the first season of the series made in Guangzhou, China. BlueArc Animation was a studio where young Chinese girls were happy to animate the Nordic IP with less violent action, and Southern Media Corporation a coproducer and a financier for 50% of the production, at a time when only a few companies were interested in growing China market.

Jim Solatie was a forerunner in many ways. With their company Futurecode, he and his wife Pia launched books with augmented reality (Figure 4.8). They have also experimented with similar technology, as the Pokémon Go app with *Dibidogs* in the Finnish archipelago a couple of seasons before the app made Japanese collectibles hugely popular again.

FIGURE 4.8 Augmented reality attached to *Dibidogs* books was a collaboration with VTT, The Finnish Research Institute, in 2010. (With permission from Futurecode/VTT.)

VALHALLA GOES VFX – THE GAMIFIED KALEVALA?

It is said that in pre-Christian times, Nordics worshipped Pagan Gods. Some of them have entered as characters in Nordic animated features. Early Danish animation hit *Valhalla* (1986) was codirected by Danish Peter Madsen and American Jeffrey James Varab. The film is based on the comic strips that have been published in the Politiken newspaper since 1978. Thor acts as the main hero in the movie where he takes small children to the land of Odin, who is Thor's father in the film but often considered the Nordic equivalent of Zeus or Ra. The other characters met are Luke and Quark. Þjálfi, or Tjalfe, and Røskva were Thor's servants in the original poetic Edda.

The film premiered at Cannes Film Festival and was shown in Los Angeles on July 11, 1987. The production was a massive effort in the mid-1980s, and it is often mentioned as the beginning of the Danish animation industry. Right after its production, the studio A. Film was born, and most talents got employed there. For example, Anders Mastrup, the CEO of A. Film, acted as an Assistant Producer in *Valhalla*, while Jørgen Lerdam was an Assistant Director. The main production company was Swan Film Production, for which it remained its only feature.

Thor: Legend of the Magical Hammer (2011) is a more recent and much more successful Icelandic CG animated movie, made in 3D. The magical weapon that Thor possesses plays a very important role in the film. One could think that the gun has its equivalent in Finnish *Kalevala's* Sampo, which is a magical device constructed by the blacksmith Ilmarinen. There was a belief that Sampo would bring riches and good fortune to its holder.

Finnish national epic *Kalevala* has its god-like characters too. A few ambitious attempts have been made to take those into the big screen as an animated feature, but, so far, the Soviet–Finnish live action from 1959 remains a rare example. Its American title is *The Day the Earth Froze*. *Kalevala* is visually interesting and definitely has many characters that could be developed into an animation.

Nordic Digital Film Company, or NDFC, was a production company founded by Kare and Veera Hellén. Kare had worked as a CEO for Talvi Productions, which did high-quality 3D animation commercials in Helsinki. He had been following the success of Niko films and hired their director Kari Juusonen to develop the ambitious project with the screenwriter Leo Viirret, both student fellows.

The company aimed not to produce only one feature-length film but a trilogy based on the stories of *Kalevala* called *Aurora Nord*. The first film in the series was supposed to be titled *The Sampo*. It got development support from the Finnish Film foundation worth 90,000 Euros. The film was marketed for its influence on J.R.R. Tolkien's *Lord of the Rings* and *Silmarillion* works (Figure 4.9).

When the project was pitched at Cartoon Movie, Dreamworks Europe representative Shelley Page criticized it for bringing the game aesthetics into the animation world. Kare Hellén found a few partners in China and Austria, but the project was suddenly given up. There were rumors that somebody ran away with the development money or spent them just too fast. The test animations were made in Asia, not in Finland, and people in the industry criticized that for taking the subsidy money out from the country.

The second big-scale attempt to animate the legends of Kalevala was announced at the Slush start-up event in 2014. At that time, the event was growing huge, both in popularity and media attention. The teaser for *Iron Danger* had been made by Rovio and Supercell employees during their working hours and shown to journalists visiting Slush. Some key members of the team, Sami Timonen and Jussi Kemppainen, were both working at Studio Kombo, while it was acquired by Rovio. They got supported by Peter Vesterbacka, once the loud spokesperson for the game company in those days. Vesterbacka was no animation expert, but he was good at pretending to be both an inventor and acting like a superstar in some animation festivals in China.

NDFC Helsinki & The Sampo Trilogy

KALEVALA GETS ANIMATED
THE EPIC THAT INSPIRED *J.R.R. TOLKIEN*

The Sampo is a feature-length 3D stereoscopic animation based on the ancient Finnish epic, Kalevala. It is the 1st episode of the stereoscopic AURORA NORD TRILOGY.

AURORA NORD is the narrator in the film trilogy, digital media and social media content. She can travel through time and space to distant places and tell the tales of the ancient Nordic lands.

CONTACT:
NDFC Helsinki Oy
Kristianinkatu 1 A 1
00170 Helsinki,
FINLAND

Kare Hellén, CEO,
Executive Producer
kare.hellen@ndfc.fi
+358 400 808 548

FORMAT:
A trilogy of 3 feature films
TARGET AUDIENCE:
Young people (at least
young in their minds)
GENRE:
Adventure, fantasy
BUDGET:
Approximately 10 M€
FUNDING:
From Europe, Asia and
Russia.

STATUS:
First draft script, concept trailer and first
pictures of the main characters ready.
TIMETABLE:
By the end of 2010, all key art will have been developed and produced.

THE CORE TEAM:
Aurora Nord and The Sampo are created by NDFC
Helsinki Oy. The company was founded in late 2006 in
Helsinki, Finland and is privately owned by Kare Hellén
and Veera Hellén.

Director: Kari Juusonen
(Niko - Way to the Stars, Pizza Passionata)
CG-supervisor and creative producer: Martin Jäger
Character designer: Sami Saramäki
Original film treatment by Ian Gray,
Kare Hellén and Veera Hellén
Script 1.0 by Leo Viiret
Linguist and English translator: Robert Brooks

WWW.AURORANORD.ORG

Finland has the largest collection of ancient myths in the world. Many of these myths are re-told in the pages of *Kalevala*. Numerous writers, including J.R.R. Tolkien, have understood the power of these old legends and stories. In fact, any film based on Kalevala could easily be promoted as an adaptation of "The Inspiration for the *The Lord of the Rings*".

J.R.R. Tolkien used material from Kalevala in all of his novels, but especially in *The Lord of the Rings* and The *Silmarillion*. He even learnt the Finnish language to be able to read *Kalevala* in the original language.

"*Kalevala* is written in old Finnish. It took us two years to translate it into modern Finnish and then into English," says producer Kare Hellén from NDFC Helsinki Oy. "We used professional writers, translators and a linguist in the translation process because of the outstanding requirements of the project. We hold the publishing rights and the copyright of this new version."

DID YOU KNOW THAT...
Eight of the all-time worldwide box office Top Ten movies are adventure and fantasy movies. Among the most popular of these are Star Wars, The Lord of the Rings, Harry Potter, World of Warcraft and Narnia. The Lord of the Rings trilogy is the second most sold book in the world ever – number one is the Bible.

Concept art picture of giant wizard Antero Vipunen.

Map of Kalevala and Pohjola.

FIGURE 4.9 Kalevala animations have got boosted by the success of J.R.R. Tolkien's *Lord of the Rings* saga. (Courtesy of Finnanimation.)

The big Kalevala animation was to be released to celebrate Finland's 100th anniversary year in 2017 but remains to be seen if that ever happens. Its fantasy design was later turned into a video game, which was released in March 2020.

Jarmo Lampela, Head of Drama at YLE since 2015, said in his interview for this book that he warmly welcomes adult-oriented animation for YLE. Instead of Kalevala-themed which he finds

FIGURE 4.10 Belzebubs series is beautifully crafted in black and white ink. It will be directed by Samppa Kukkonen, who partners Terhi Väänänen in Turku based Pyjama Films studio, founded in 2015. (With permission from Pyjama Films + J.P.Ahonen.)

problematic, his next commission, after *Moominvalley* and *Divine Consultants* web series, is *Belzebubs* series (Figure 4.10) adapted from J.P.Ahonen's popular comic. Belzebubs is a family sitcom documenting the lives of your average devil worshiping family next door, their romantic affairs and the sluggish evolution of the father's hapless black metal band. I agree with Lampela that the poetic nature of Kalevala would be a challenge to adapt beautifully as it is in the ancient language where the value of the epic poetry lies, not in progressive present-day heroes. The alliteration typical to Kalevala's verses works excellent in an audio book. The big mistake, practiced often in the game aesthetics, is to pixelate stories into the overall darkness and therefore hiding wrong pixels.

Telling about the Nordic elves to the contemporary international audience might also fail. You have to balance your writings with some people who still want to think of them as genuine. Rituals still occur among some new age or Neo-Pagan subcultures, and they seem to strengthen rather than disappear. These days, you ought to believe in natural rather than Christian belief exported to the North by some past kings and queens.

Iceland is still a country where the majority of people would rather believe in elves than gods. Some roads have taken another route if an elf is thought to live there. Having been to Iceland only once as a tourist, I got powerful mystical feelings in Thingvellir national park, where the North American and Eurasian tectonic plates move away from each other. There is an old cemetery too, and you have the same intense feeling of being surrounded by curious spirits in some cemeteries.

The fact that the earth is splitting apart in the middle of Iceland makes it an exciting place to live. The site is in constant motion, so to say. The change happens with the glaciers melting and volcanic eruption reshaping the land. People often reason that demanding conditions are likely to explain that you might feel the presence of God or gods. On the top of the mountain, or by the seashore of the very remote place, that happens too.

Although Nordics share the same mythological landscape, as a Finnish woman I feel a bit alienated from the Viking sagas, specially how they are put in VFX productions. Genetically many Finnish, including those who had to exile from Karelia after World War II, belong to the Viking tribe. Tall blondes with blue eyes are also found in Russia and the Baltics, if not Northern America, where many of our fore-uncles and fore-aunts have immigrated.

One reason why various types of gods are written into the old legends may alianate, not just me but the contemporary audience of films and series is that adaptations often take those that represent the most masculine or the most feminine characteristics. So parallel to Thor, who is described as a big manly fighter with some superpowers, Freya is characterized for love and beauty from American Marvel to Japanese anime.

Most recently, Viking legends with gods and kings have been material to mega VFX productions made outside the Nordics. Although some VFX experts born in Nordic countries work in those, the stories and artistic direction are made by others to match the expectations of the older target audience that is typical to most animations. However, new heroes can be made from totally different perspective, as will be written in the next chapters with more studio stories and case studies with their recent success stories.

CHAPTER 5

Making New Heroes

MOSVOLD GOES INTERNATIONAL

Among the current animation filmmakers in Norway, Frank Mosvold (Figure 5.1) is one of the most original. He names Ivo Caprino as his main influencer with no hesitation: "Caprino's *Flåklypa Grand Prix* (*The Pinchcliffe Grand Prix*, 1975) just blew me away when I saw the film in the cinema as a 10 year old. I started making my own puppet animation in our basement with my dad's Super-8 camera."

When Frank is asked about his opinion about Nordic animation, his kind and open-minded nature picks up many valuable Danish and Finnish executives who have helped him in building up his international career. Frank is in awe of both the *Niko* films: "I admired the ambition and risks taken. They were impressive pictures with superb international-style marketing campaigns."

"We have to think of the Nordic countries as one market, as our home market. We have to label and sell our films internationally as Nordic films. We have to help each other, if we want to grow outside our small countries!" Frank says. He is forever grateful to Finnish Pii Berg from YLE for giving him the

FIGURE 5.1 Frank Mosvold (left) celebrating his first sales with Finnish producers Nick Dorra (middle) and Jim Solatie (right) in Annecy in 2009. (Image provided by the author.)

first international Letter Of Intent in Annecy 2009 for the series *Ella Bella Bingo* (2009–2015, original release on NRK): "With her support, our *Ella Bella Bingo* idea became a TV series and later a trans-media universe with books, toys, interactive games, and finally in 2020 a 3D feature. Without her help, there would not have been an *Ella Bella Bingo*" (Figure 5.2).

With the help of coproducer August Media Holding in Singapore and the renowned distributor Cake Entertainment in

FIGURE 5.2 *Ella Bella Bingo* (2020) feature followed the success of the series created by Frank Mosvold. (With permission from Kool Production AS.)

London, the 2D Flash animated TV series sold to multiple territories, around 40 countries, from Indonesia to Turkey.

The *Ella Bella Bingo* TV series was created by Tom Petter Hansen, Trond Morten Venaasen, and Frank. "Our goal was actually to make a feature from the start. At first, we wanted to make a few TV episodes as a proof of concept but ended up making 104 episodes of 7 minutes each." The TV series was directed by Ginger Gibbons, while the story editor was Sam Barlow. The series follows the adventures of 5-year-old Ella and her many friends. The main character using her boundless creativity and infectious enthusiasm solving everyday problems affectionately melts hearts. The idea is basic but works, spreading happiness in focus.

According to Frank, good children's content is when the young audience connects and identifies with the heroes of the movie and television screens. Nordic literature and entertainment take children seriously. "It's fantastic how the Swedish author Astrid Lindgren looks at the world from the child's point of view."

When the *Ella Bella Bingo* television series was first broadcasted, there was a lack of children's content with strong female characters—single parents in multicultural and contemporary settings. Ten years ago, most Nordic animation was based on books and stories from 1940s and 1950s. "The stories were progressive when they came out, but not so much today. We have to make contemporary stories for contemporary kids!"

The development of the *Ella Bella Bingo* feature version started in 2013. The film was written by Frank Mosvold and the writing duo Rob Sprackling and Johnny Smith (famously known for *Gnomeo & Juliet* (2011) and *The Queen's Corgi* (2019)). Mike de Seve and his team at Baboon Animation in New York City served as story consultants.

The film's official budget, 6 million Euros, a bit behind the two Finnish *Niko* films but ahead most Nordic features, could have done much better commercially without the unfortunate COVID-19 lockdowns around the globe. The *Ella Bella Bingo* movie had been sold to more than 100 countries by Studio 100 in Germany, but good marketing campaigns did not help much when the cinemas were closed and people had to stay at home. In Sweden, all the cinemas closed the day the film premiered; in Belgium, it could only be seen for three days; and, in France and the USA, the film went immediately to VOD and DVD. The US celebrity cast includes Summer Fontana (*Dark Phoenix*), Richard Kind (several Pixar movies), and Tress MacNeille (*Simpsons, Futurama*).

In the home market the *Ella Bella Bingo* feature premiered on January 24, 2020 and was ranked fourth (biggest selling film) behind three Hollywood blockbusters on its opening week. By the beginning of April 2020, the number of Norwegian theaters, starting with 161, dropped to three due to COVID-19. In Denmark, the film was one of the most popular Norwegian family films until the theaters closed again because of COVID-19. In Iceland, the film went to number one during its first week and hold the position between the five best selling theatrical films until mid-September 2020. Russian success was a remarkable surprise, and it got many unexpected fans as well in South Korea. 2021 premieres included Spain with 159 theaters in major Spanish cities, and, in 2022, the film opened nationwide with more countries to follow (IMDbPro).

The *Ella Bella Bingo* feature was produced by Frank Mosvold's Kool Produktion and coproduced with Torgeir Sanders of Gimpville. The Norwegian coproducer is well known for special effects on many live-action films, including *Trollhunter* (2010), and wanted to expand into feature animation. Gimpville did the animation together with A.Film in Copenhagen, and with animators from all the Nordic countries and Mexico. Frank Mosvold's choice of codirector was Atle Solberg Blakseth after their successful codirection of their popular animated short film *Bendik & the Monster*.

When asked why Frank makes movies and TV series about a 5-year-old girl, he laughs; "I think I am a girl at heart. At least, I am a child at heart. I could never imagine making mass-murder movies or anything like that. We are all humans with childish joy. All we want is to play and be loved," Frank explains.

Frank is respected by his Norwegian colleagues (Figure 5.3), as he was the first one to started looking for the international audience as well as foreign financing and worldwide distribution both for the series and the feature film. Born into a wealthy Norwegian shipping family, he was raised to have an international perspective. Frank left Kristiansand, his hometown on the south coast of Norway, to study Economics in New York when he was 19. After his business study and 4 years as a broker in New York and London, he realized he was not content. He moved to Hollywood to come out of the closet and to study cinema in Los Angeles. He stayed in the USA for 12 years: "At film school, I wanted to be the new Ingmar Bergman. My first short films were existential movies dealing with gender, identity, and sexuality. In the beginning, I used film as a therapy, says Frank Mosvold." He told his parents that he was gay by screening

FIGURE 5.3 It was Frank Mosvold's initiative to gather Nordic producers to have a mutual booth in Mifa market since 2017. Katariina Lillqvist
(in the center) won the prize for the best music that year for the music in
Radio Dolores short film. (Image provided by the author.)

them his first student film, *Forsaken*. His early films are still very
popular. His live-action short—*Bølgene* (*Waves*, 1998) is his most
personal film and has about 1.5 million views on his YouTube
channel—*Frankie Sunshine*. "I guess, I have ended up being the
children's Ingmar Bergman," Frank laughs.

Frank Mosvold's quest to make a feature film has been long. It
was a dream he had already in film school. After having moved
back to Norway, he wrote and directed *Summer Blues* in 2002.
Frank says the film was meant to be a feature, but in the editing he
realized the story was not strong enough. "The film was cut down
to 25 minutes, and I felt like a failure. My goal to make a feature
film had collapsed. I was sitting in my studio being depressed and
feeling bad for myself, when accidentally, a 19-year-old boy, Tom
Petter Hansen, came to my office and suggested we should make

animation. I remembered the joy I had making animation as a kid. Together, we made two Flash animated shorts. One was an anti-George Bush movie and the other was about a 16-year-old gay boy with a small penis. Both films became wildly successful festival hits. At one festival Tone C Rønning from NRK, the Norwegian public service broadcaster, happened to see it and wanted to work with us. This is how we end up doing 26 episodes of our first animated TV-series *Hubert*."

In June 2022, Mosvold was pitching his new feature film, *The Legend of Magnus the Good*, in Annecy. Here he wants to combine the theme of his early personal films with family animation. The film is about a young Viking prince, who travels in time and ends up with three drag queens in present day Norway. Frank is also developing the poetic feature *Magical Friends* with Ulvenfilm, another Norwegian production company that has made animated shorts since 2016.

Frank Mosvold has been on the board of the Kristiansand International Children Film Festival since 2007. The festival is one of the biggest children film festivals in Northern Europe. Kristiansand is also well known in Scandinavia for Kristiansand Dyrepark, in English known as Kristiansand Zoo and Amusement Park. Frank's uncle, Tor Bjørn Mosvold, was one of the founding fathers for it. The park is a home for the fictional *Kardemomme By, Cardamom* Town in English, and the pirate show *Kaptein Sabeltann* (*Captain Sabertooth* in English) premiered in 1990 and still going strong. Both the universes have been translated into animated features by Qvisten—the biggest Nordic animation studio in Oslo and in Nordics too.

QVISTEN FOLLOWS

At the time of Cartoon Forum held in Stavanger in 2009, Qvisten was already a major Norwegian production studio but mainly satisfying the domestic needs for animation. It had no international strategy in the same natural choice as Frank Mosvold, but it has to go outside its frontiers in 12 years. By the end of 2021, Qvisten had 70 employees.

Global perspectives have been opened with some new financing structures. For streaming services, it does not matter where the content comes, but you have to be creative and efficient. Efficiency is one of the assets for the Norwegian studio, exactly the same way as for Finnish Anima Vitae or Danish A. Film.

According to the director Rasmus A. Sivertsen (b. 1972), whose father was making experimental animation at the time Rasmus was toddling; the number of features made in Qvisten, going up to 20 in total, is the result of its efficiency. "For sure, you have to keep budgets lower than in average European animated features," the director for most of these films confirms (Figure 5.4).

On delivery times, the Qvisten can make animated commercials in 3 weeks; from a feature film, it takes from them approximately 2 years. During the first 8 or 10 years, Oslo-based company did mostly commercials.

Both the director and producer Ove Heiborg—the spiritual head of the company—think that in an international context they want to make stories from all the Nordic countries and keep the Nordic touch. "We share the same culture, and there are numerous untold stories ready to move out. Even the smallest stories can be adapted into interesting films," they whisper.

In Norway, there is a lot of talent to be found these days. Many people actually ask why you have a studio in the country located so North and expensive. Ove admits that it is a constant struggle, but their decision has proved to be right. After 27 production years, they still have the studio in their own hands, and the personnel is very passionate in working both with new and classical titles (Figure 5.5).

Interestingly, half of the people working in Qvisten are not Norwegians. There are specially many Swedish people who have crossed the border and moved to Norway after better salaries. In some stop-motion productions, there has been around 15 different nationalities among the crew. Bulgarian and Brazil employees might be the most exotic ones.

Gender structure inside the studio has been changing from the majority of guys 10 years ago to a good balance with half-women

FIGURE 5.4   Rasmus A. Sivertsen is one of the most efficient Nordic directors. In 2022, the studio had three premieres, including *Just Super*, which was presented at Cartoon Movie 2022. (Courtesy of Cartoon.)

FIGURE 5.5 Kristiansand Zoo and Amusement Park has been a home for the pirate show *Kaptein Sabeltann* (*Captain Sabertooth* in English) since 1990. The animation feature by Qvisten premiered in 2019. (With permission from Qvisten Animation.)

and half-men. Nonidentical productions need all kinds of personalities.

All Qvisten productions have been made completely in Norway. That is not the cheapest way, but affordable. The highest budget for a feature has been 5,500,000 Euros for a mix of stop-motion and Computer Generated Imagery (CGI). In Norway, the local funding can be raised up to 4–5 million Euros, but a coproducing model is a way to raise the budget.

Tax incentive for Norway was launched in January 2016. For the first year, the amount of funding available was set at 5,000,000 Euros, which was quickly taken by two live-action companies and commented by the Norwegian film professionals being far too low.

According to the study made on the Norwegian incentive, screen tourism impacts are a key benefit. This phenomenon has been measured in a few studies producing a value of between 116 and 162 million Euros. "A number of films, including animated Disney blockbuster movie *Frozen*, already have anecdotal evidence of tourism impacts in Norway, demonstrating the potential for such downstream value creation across a range of different productions, including one not created in the country. *The Snowman* would be expected to generate similar impacts, akin to *The Killing* and *The Bridge* in Copenhagen, both of which have generated strong tourism benefits for the local economy and been instrumental in the reframing of the Copenhagen tourism offer within Europe." (Olsberg SPi, 2017, p. 13). Interesting thing found in the 2017 study is that attracting VFX-only projects should also be considered, "as these will use skills already in the country and are also often possibly given the 80% budget cap for incentives under the European Union's Cinema Communication" (Anon, Olsberg SPi, 2017).

Considering the challenge of marketing so many titles, Ove and Rasmus think that they use clients to market their films. Sponsors, like the theme park in Kristiansand, have been collaborating in four films. A Disney effect, after *Frozen*'s impact in Norway, can be seen in how Norwegian travel industry with their attractions eagerly promote films.

Both Rasmus A. and Ove remember the time when there was no interest on Norwegian TV stations in local animation. A big change happened with the popularity of streaming platforms. As the competition with them is pushing broadcasters into more tight position, the quality has to be guaranteed with the cooperation between national channels.

Qvisten was one of five studios collaborating in a TV special commissioned by Norwegian NRK, Danish DR, Icelandic RÚV, and Finnish YLE in Christmas 2022. The project, being both ambitious and asking a lot from studio, was called *Nordic Christmas Hour*. Its grand idea is to replace the Disney block—the tradition that has been on all Nordic TV channels since the very first years of television in the 1950s.

Making a truly Nordic Christmas means that the most immortal stories of Astrid Lindgren, Kjell Aukrust, and H.C. Andersen were be part of it as well as adorable Moomins. The Danish studio that collaborated in the project is Happy Flyfish. In Finland, the collaboration is done with Gigglebug . The show premiered on NRK and RÚV at 10 a.m. on Dec. 24, 2022. On Yle it had two shows: on TV2 on Dec. 24, 2022 right after noon with Finnish dubbing and on Yle Fem later in the evening with Swedish dubbbing. DR had the show at 7 p.m. on Dec. 25, 2022.

Another big and awaited hit landed in Norwegian cinemas in Christmas 2022 was the adaptation of Thorbjørn Egner's *Folk og røvere i Kardemomme By* with the English name *Three Robbers and a Lion*. It is also directed by Rasmus A. Sivertsen, and it is produced by Qvisten Animation with Heidi Palm Sandberg and Åshild Ramborg as producers (Figures 5.6 and 5.7).

FIGURE 5.6 Thorbjørn Egner (1912–1990) was a Norwegian cartoonist, author, songwriter, and composer. His name should be mentioned along with more famous Danish, Swedish, and Finnish children's book authors. (Courtesy of Oslo Museum.)

FIGURE 5.7 *Three Robbers and a Lion* present the most famous characters created by Thorbjørn Egner. Villains look for acceptance by the people living in the Cardamom Town by becoming a rescue team in a fire. (With permission from Qvisten Animation.)

One of the key messages in a new adaptation is: *You shall never bother others. You shall be both fair and kind. And whatever else you do I surely shall not mind.* In a story about three robbers Casper, Jasper, and Jonathan, who live outside Cardamom Town, they would like to live as normal people. After robbing the town several times, they are finally caught and put in jail. When a fire breaks out in the tower of the town, the robbers come to help and become heroes of the day. Distributor is Nordisk Film, and a sales agent is Sola Media.

To my question about comparing Nordic countries in animation business, Ove and Rasmus would like to remind of Sweden's glorious past: "They are still very good at 2D animation. Happy Life was much known for a while, in making both features and TV series; but it must be their funding system that has not created animated blockbusters," they say by referring to the superiority of the Norwegian system. "It is just better."

An important support schemes, which many Norwegian animation productions have benefited, is "ex post support" that is received by all feature films and documentaries that have sold a minimum of 10,000 or 35,000 tickets through ordinary theatrical release in Norway. It is semiautomatic, based on sales revenue from all release windows during the 3 years following the first release.

If Norway has not yet seen an equal triumph as Finland and Sweden with the game industry or the VFX sector, the animation industry does not have to worry so much for those eating the talent from it. Animations in Norway's neighbors are struggling both with long development times and sufficient financing. Late 1990s was also hard times in Norway. Many earlier studios disappeared, and only some individual talent remained doing shorts as individual projects.

Qvisten has also collaborated with the Icelandic studio Caoz. With Danish studio Hydralab, they dared to touch Astrid Lindgren's christmas story and made a stop-motion short *The Tomten and the Fox (Reven og Nissen)* in 2019.

The stop-motion film *In the Forest of Huckybucky* (*Dyrene I Hakkebakkeskogen,* 2016), which is based on the classic novel by Thorbjørn Egner, was done with the Netherlands. The story has many cute animals from mice to rabbits, and predators that are threatening and eating them. When the hedgehog tries to eat the mouse grandma, it is time to stop the lawlessness. Jens Petersen, the film critic from Aftonbladet, said in his review that the film contains cleverly built dramaturgy. Many captivating songs have already been sung for several generations, but they have been arranged in a jazz style in the film from 2016, sometimes resembling New Orleans tunes (Figure 5.8).

"Stop-motion films are very popular in France. They are interested in its technique," Ove says. Qvisten has also found new audience for their films in China. One of their films had already a quota, allowing it to be shown in Chinese cinemas; but it waits to be seen how the pandemic still affects the Eastern superpower.

FIGURE 5.8 *In the Forest of Huckybucky* (Dyrene i Hakkebakkeskogen, 2016) mice, who are always scared of getting eaten by predators, make new laws so that all animals could live in peace. The film embraces and respects diversity in a funny and entertaining. (With permission from Qvisten Animation.)

NEW SCHOOL VIBORG: NØRLUM AND DANISH DOCUMENTARY ANIMATION

Eighty kilometers north of the LEGO headquarters, there is a small town Viborg with around 40,000 inhabitants. In the old army barracks, left behind by the Royal Danish Army in 2001, is one of the Europe's best animation schools—The Animation Workshop. The school, founded already in 1988, has more variety in courses and levels than other Nordic animation schools. The Animation Workshop belongs to the VIA University College— one of the biggest polytechnics in Denmark and headquartered in Århus, the capital of Jutland (Figure 5.9).

The environment is otherwise idyllic but darkened by the 19th-century military past, if not Hitler's occupation too during the Second World War. Have to say, there are more picturesque Scandinavian cities, once visited a small town with its famous school. However, the level of education and its variety has

FIGURE 5.9 Viborg is a small town in Northern Jylland. Its houses have been removed from their military use for The Animation Workshop—VIA College, ranked the 7th best animation school in the world. (Image provided by the author.)

attracted both hard working and ambitious people to concentrate on their animation studies here.

The school has also fed the start-up scene, where one of the most successful stories is that of Nørlum. Under the leadership of producer Claus Toksvig Kjaer, director Frederic Villumsen, based in Copenhagen, and third partner Jericca Cleland, based in Vancouver, Nørlum has got a chance to work with Irish, French, American, and eventually with talented Norwegian and Swedish colleagues.

In 2015, Nørlum's first-ever coproduction *Song of the Sea* was nominated for Best Animated Film at the Oscars. Since this first-ever Oscar nomination in animated features hitting a Nordic country, Nørlum has found specialized work with American studios and museums. However, even the nomination promises, Nørlum belongs to the studios that can do the task required.

"People started to want to work with you since the nomination was public; they know you. We got many more applications for our vacancies, around 650 for 17 open posts," Claus remembers. Before COVID-19 hit the Danish outskirts, the studio had around 40 to 50 people who started working from home, and some left for their home countries.

"At best, we had around 60 people working in artistic programs for American and European museums, Disney Junior, Disney XD, Amazon Prime, and 20th Century Fox," Claus says. He counts their clients feeling sorry for Warner Bros, as the timing was not good, and the intended project did not go on.

Budgets in coproductions, in which Nørlum has been participating, have been rising. Starting with the 2014 film *Song of the Sea* with the Irish Cartoon Saloon, the budget was only around 5,300,000 Euros. In a French–Danish coproduction, *Long Way North* (2015) budget rose a bit to 6 million Euros, but in *Calamity, a Childhood of Martha Jane Cannary* (2020), the budget reached 8,000,000 Euros. Both French films are directed by French Rémi Chayé—one of the most notable European animation directors (Figure 5.10).

FIGURE 5.10 *Calamity, a Childhood of Martha Jane Cannary* (2020) feature is the third international coproduction for Viborg-based 2D studio Nørlum. Having a strong female character in the film has gained good feedback worldwide. ((©) With permission from Maybe Movies–Nørlum–2 Minutes–France 3 Cinema.)

Working with Irish Tomm Moore was also an essential experience to achieve knowledge for the future projects. Tomm is super talented in handling shapes and colors, making *Song of the Sea* a unique, almost elliptical film. The tale matches with chosen forms, precisely like an embryo fitting in a womb or a pearl fitting in an oyster shell.

Danish money collected for coproductions came from the Danish Film Institute, Copenhagen Film Fund, and the regional West Danish Film Fund. According to Claus, percentages vary from case to case, but the approximate is around 15%, which Denmark can raise for financing. "If you get the maximum for one film like we did with *Long Way North*, there is a chance to raise the total budget."

Concerning the film's reception, *Long Way North* did very well in Japan. "We screened the film at Studio Ghibli, and Isao Takahata saw the film. He loved it so much that he toured with it afterwards," Claus tells. America did critically well for beautiful scenes and toning with a cold color scheme. Claus thinks that the home audience in Denmark did not find the culturally French film equally familiar, while *Song of the Sea* was received better. Often local films do not get enough marketing money from distributors. If you book big names as voice actors, it helps a bit. That was a strategy with *Calamity* with a top cast familiar from series like *Game of Thrones* or *The Killing*.

The first genuine Nordic coproduction for Nørlum was *The Ape Star* feature, which premiered at the Annecy festival in 2021. Norwegian and Danish partners were founded by Stockholm-based director Linda Hambäck and the trusted producer Petter Lindblad who managed the most stuff animated in Sweden. Lindblad gained experience in another Danish production company—Copenhagen Bombay, having started its division in Sweden. Hambäck has been one of the Swedish Film Institute's favorites, receiving support both for her TV specials and the first feature, *The Ape Star*.

"The key thing always is planning well. There is no chance to change things with Nordic projects, but we want to stick to normal working hours and keep a long summer holiday that Americans do not know anything about," Claus roars with his team (Figure 5.11).

Claus underlines that Nørlum has been a Danish company since day one. It is owned by The Animation Workshop, where it was born. Claus thinks that animation can travel if you are wise, and dubbing can add the local humor, but Danish comedy does not travel at all. "British humor is liked by many in Denmark, but it is considered rude if you try to copy it in Danish production." Danish and Norwegians have a lot in typical, but Swedish and Finnish humor are more distant.

Already at school, Claus got to work, specially with Italians and French. They got a Peruvian couple working in Denmark for his startup after spending some time in Ireland. The Argentinian guy did well too.

FIGURE 5.11   Nørlum team for *Calamity—a Childhood of Martha Jane Cannary* (2020) feature. Claus Toksvig Kjaer fourth on the right. (With permission from Nørlum.)

Competition between countries and cities can be healthy, and even many young people want to leave Viborg for Copenhagen or other countries after school in tiny Viborg. Still, many stay thanks to the supportive startup scene and students available during their internships to cut the labor cost, which are higher in Denmark than in Sweden or Finland.

Claus thinks that The Animation Workshop is the second-best animation school in Europe after the French Gobelins, l'école de l'image. Both the schools are industry ready, meaning that students are ready to work on challenging animation projects, both features and series. "When you get students from other schools, it is very likely that you have to train them first. So it slows the process."

The Animation Workshop has benefited from good teachers coming from all parts of the world. Most teachers are people from the industry, and we depend on them. Another important thing is to have the latest software taught to students. Becoming a wanted professional from the famous Danish school takes 3 years to study and 1 year more as an intern. When Claus started school, all the courses were just 1-year long. "I could have become an animator, but I was too slow. That is why I became a producer," Claus laughs. A high-profile American professional told him that he is so good with people, which is not common among animators, so he had to become a producer, and, eventually, Claus is a wanted coproducer: "I acknowledge that most producers come from live action with very unrealistic schedules."

Both Claus and Lana Tankosa Nikolic, who founded another successful company—Late Love Production, in 2016, have been working as coordinators for the Viborg school. Thus, they have had access both to the school resources and international networks. The job is about planning masterclasses and hosting teachers who come from major US studios. "It is a pretty good job when you are building your own company simultaneously," Claus admits and waves to Lana across the lawn. "Martina Scarpelli from Italy and Lana from Denmark make a great team with brilliant artistic ideas. They have traveled to numerous festivals and received many prizes," Claus vaunts his colleagues.

Late Love Production is best known for a short animation *Egg* (2018) (Figures 5.12 and 5.13). A 12-minute film made in black and white expresses a relationship between a woman and her body. More than 50 awards for the best short film, the best animated short, and the best first film from the most important festivals show that their style and vision are respected as awe-inspiring. Coproduced with French Miyu Productions, the collaboration evidences the working relationship between the Nordic country and the French for their part. France Télévisions supported the short film. However, making money as a producer of short films is difficult, if not impossible. The making of *Egg* took 4 years.

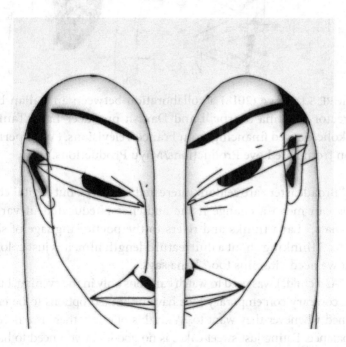

FIGURE 5.12 Feminist movie *Egg* (2018) by Martina Scarpelli is examining a woman's relationship with her body. (With permission of Late Love Productions / Miyu Producions.)

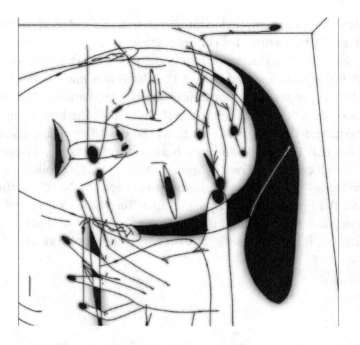

FIGURE 5.13 *Egg* (2018) a collaboration between an Italian-born director Martina Scarpelli and Danish producer Lana Tankasa Nikolic, gained financing from France Télévisions. (With permission from Late Love Productions/Miyu Productions.)

"Broadcasters are seldom interested in shorts, but digital channels can mean a change if the audience is educated in various formats," Lana thinks and refers to the poetic language of short films. "Thinking about a dull feature-length film, it is just calories, but we need vitamins too," Lana says.

"As a child, I was used to watch cartoons only in the evening, but on the contrary contemporary kids have unlimited options to be entertained whenever they want to. With this offering, there is a need for a balance. Eating just sweet cakes is no good, but you need to have a choice for rye bread," Lana explains her premises as a shorts producer.

Late Love Production has also been active in developing an animated opera, some animated documentaries with Michelle and Uri Kranot, and even VR projects.

"Making VR is less elastic; you have to fit it in different venues," says the producer who has educated herself in theater, photography, and live-action films. "I was good at facilitating things, it made me a producer."

The next Viborg-born company with high expectations in the future is Sun Creature. They have already left the school premises to Copenhagen and opened a studio in France for a series production. Their most famous work at the Danish studio is the animated documentary *Flee* (2021), which was nominated at the Oscars in three categories. In Nordic and European competitions, it got several wins.

Ouros Animation was started by Rikke Planeta and Philip Piaget in October 2020. Despite the short history, they have already released a series project with Parka Pictures, a Copenhagen-based production company, which started as an offspring of A. Film's most esteemed project and has already established a sister company in Germany after many coproductions with Denmark's southern neighbor.

Both the companies, Ouros Animation and Parka Pictures, are developing also computer-generated (CGI) animated feature. It happens in a long, long winter, so dark and so icy cold that hopeless animals are feeling profoundly winter blue. There will be snowy monsters sent by the winter king and a brave little bear who must save his friend before he hibernates.

FROM FILMTECKNARNA TO LEE FILM AND *THE APE STAR*

Filmtecknarna started as a collective with independent 2D artists whose visual ambition was wider from television graphics to music videos a bit like Happy Life. Swedish "cartoonists" were the most active in the 1990s, benefiting from the boom of new commercial tv channels TV3 and TV4. In 2005, the studio had around

FIGURE 5.14 *The Ape Star* is a Swedish animated feature with Denmark and Norway coproducing. It premiered in Annecy 2021. (With permission from LEE Film.)

10 to 15 international clients commissioning various shorts, giving name to some most active animators (Marko-Nord, 2005, p. 8). If Happy Life survived without a bankruptcy, as has been told to me several times, it was Filmtecknarna, who sadly had to go due to the financial cuts and close its operations in 2011 (Figure 5.14).

Linda Hambäck (b. 1974) was working Filmtecknarna for 5 years, producing shorts for Jonas Odell, one of their talented creators, and making commercials. Since she founded her own company LEE Film in 2011, she has focused on innovative animation for the youngest audience. After six shorts and the first feature, the Nordic Noir movie for kids *Gordon and Paddy* (2017), her second feature, *The Ape Star* (*Apstjärnan*, 2021), had its Stockholm premiere in June 2021.

In an unusual mother–daughter relationship, a gorilla visits an orphanage and becomes little Jonna's new mother. The film raises serious questions about different sorts of families and being an outsider of society, but it is also a heartwarming tale based on a book by contemporary writer Frida Nilsson (b. 1979). Nilsson has made many novels with animals and humans side by side, in the same world. In France, Nilsson was awarded with the Les Olympiades literary prize in 2013. The script was written by Janne Vierth (b. 1965), who also made the film adaption of *Gordon and Patty*. Producer Petter Lindblad (b. 1975) run Swedish branch of CPH Sverige for the Danish owners in 2011–2014 before founding his own Swedish company Snowcloud Films. Gorilla foster mother was voice acted by Pernilla August.

With the total 35 M Swedish Crowns financing from Swedish Film Institute, Film I Väst fund, SVT, and LEE Film's second feature format overtakes *Metropia*. Coproducers from neighboring countries, Norway and Denmark bringing cofunding from their national institutes, and DR in Denmark were important. Pannational financiers include Nordisk Film & TV Fund and Creative Europe. "It is my first coproduction, and I think both Mikrofilm and Nørlum are dream companies to work with."

The Ape Star was first shown in Berlin in the market series. The film premiered internationally in competition at Annecy International Animation Film Festival. "In summer 2021, Annecy was just a small festival, but all went well and the atmosphere was so lovely," recalls Linda. "Many French interviews were made to promote the film having a French premiere in September," Linda told in summer 2021.

The film was also nominated for European Film Awards, where it ended up in a very challenging company with Tomm Moore's *Wolfwalkers*, and Danish *Flee* catching the prize in December 2021. In Oulu, Finland, Linda received the European Children's Film Association (ECFA) Award by the international jury. *The Ape Star* festival circuit continued and got several awards, Filmfest Hamburg (winner of MICHEL Film Award), Schlingel International Film Festival (winner of Club of Festivals Award), Gijón International Film Festival (winner of the Best Children Film Audience award), just to mention a few.

Hambäck thinks that animated TV series are impossible to finance in Sweden. There is a national budget just for one animated feature film per year and some shorts. With LEE Film she has been lucky in having a possibility to make both features and shorts, seven films in 10 years in total. In the future, there will be more and different platforms, and it is a good question whether Nordic institutes can keep up with the demand that will allow the growth in everyone's lips.

"If Dogma films in Denmark had the momentum, the same can happen with Nordic Animation. Everything just has to go like a train," Linda describes the potential, "Animation world is small, and crossing borders is possible. Animation people are friendly to one another. We are like creative marathon runners."

According to her, genre for animation could be very wide, but not in Sweden. Special effects and computer games sector are growing in many Swedish cities. "There is Haymaker in Gothenburg and Important Looking Pirates in Stockholm that are gaining support from investors," Linda lists.

Linda's third feature is already in development, but she would also like to make other formats. She thinks that the format length would also vary more, thanks to the streamers. Swedish students who graduate from animation schools easily move to the gaming industry, where they get the comfort zone with a full-time salary, some go to work with international companies. "That's sad, but it all comes down to the fact that the feature animation industry is too small in Sweden. We hope for that to change."

"We had around 150 people on the credit list, working on and with *The Ape Star*. Dockhus Animation in Trollhättan had around 20 people on board, animators, in-betweeners, and clean-up and compositing artists," Linda lists.

Music is an element in Swedish animation to be notified even in tiny shorts. In LEE film, there is a composer working in every film. "In animated films, the music is really a key element of the creation of the film; it will be part of the texture, the tone, the look. In the old days in Sweden everybody in school learned an instrument, but the art education has unfortunately become less important for our government. I worry if Sweden is becoming too much an engineer land with other sorts of values, the music which has been a Swedish trademark, could change to worse. We are not like France, where philosophy and arts are very important heritage still. My dream is that we should move towards France values, when it comes to general education."

Linda tells that French have proposed her coproduction deals, but she finds it easier to work with the neighbors. "Nordic animation is definitely developing into the industry, where more collaboration will be done. Trollhättan studios are closer to Oslo, and in Malmö they benefit from being so close to Copenhagen," Linda sees. "In Nordics we share the same work culture and language, so it's less barriers," she thinks. She would hope her company to become known as the Cartoon Saloon of Nordic with strong original IPs and creativity shown in them both visual and story wise (Figure 5.15).

THINKING BIG FROM THE BEGINNING: GIGGLEBUG ENTERTAINMENT

Anttu Harlin, CEO of the successful Gigglebug Entertainment IP studio, studied Theater and Visual Arts at The University of Brighton. He made some performance and video art for a brief period but was soon recruited in London to do special effects in a film company. After returning to Finland, his one-man studio made music videos.

Eventually, he heard that Taivas ad agency is putting up a start-up with a big vision in 2005. "They hired four people: one animator Mikko Vormala, who later founded Piñata studio; two designers, Jaakko Syvänen and Eliza Jäppinen; and me doing edit and effects," Harlin recalls.

During the second year in Character Business, the third designer Joonas Utti joined the company (Figure 5.16), assisting Vormala in the beginning. From here on Harlin and Utti have worked together, becoming one of the most talented pairs in Nordic animation. For Harlin, Nordic is the right term to go across the national borders and spreading open mindedness.

FIGURE 5.15 Linda Hambäck has been successful in receiving grants from Swedish Film Institute for her films animated nicely in 2D and discussing important family issues. (With permission of LEE Film / Anna Simonsson.)

FIGURE 5.16   Finnish duo Anttu Harlin and Joonas Utti has proved talented both in business and creatively. (With permission from Gigglebug Entertainment.)

Character Business was short lived. However, for such a short period, they did trailers and pilot episodes for imaginary series animated in Danish A. Film's sister company A Film Estonia in Tallinn. The company even started an internet portal called Kowaii TV to launch anime influenced series created in the studio (Leinonen, 2014, pp. 464–465).

Experience in working such in ambitious yet crazy environment taught Anttu and Joonas to set up their goal as high as possible. When Character Business got closed by its owners, the team bolstered with Eliza in those days decided to continue on the same basis at their own company. For the new start-up, they needed to get a loan from the bank and asked both Fake Graphics, the company where the other major CB designers Mikko Vormala and Jaska Syvänen first moved, and Anima Vitae to guarantee it.

"In Anima, they liked our 2D designs, as they were the best 3D studio at that time in Northern Europe. So that is how the collaboration started, and Anima Boutique was founded as a sister company," tells Harlin.

Years that Anima Vitae and Anima Boutique shared in the post-industrial wasteland next to wholesale halls and storages in the eastern downtown proved to be a creative period. Making commercials was still profitable and gave extra cash for developing concepts, having joyous parties, and traveling a lot. Harlin did already made a career leap in Character Business from a compositor to a production manager and a producer (Leinonen, 2014, p. 465), and started presenting projects in Los Angeles, where his uncle Renny Harlin worked as a film director.

At Anima Boutique, Eliza, Joonas, and Anttu worked hard on making and producing commercials for Finnish and international retail brands. Jäppinen finished her first, anime-influenced short film *Love in the Mountains* in 2009 commissioned by Helsinki International Film Festival for its trailer (Figure 5.17). We screened it to the Japanese audience in 2012, who were devoted Finland fans and curious about the differences recognizably Finnish not Japanese. Some of Eliza's ideas in motion, like liquid things running over the face of Cherry, the fictional character for the virtual band Studio Killers, have been mastered by Jani Kuronen—the leading 3D wizard in Anima Vitae. According to Eliza, the character was created to comment against the glorification of thinness (Leinonen, 2014, p. 469).

FIGURE 5.17 Eliza Jäppinen directed her first short *Love in the Mountains* as a trailer for the Helsinki International Film Festival, mixing different Japanese styles from arts, manga, and anime. Characters are designed by Joonas Utti. (With permission from Joonas Utti and Eliza Jäppinen.)

Strong interest in character development took both Eliza and Anttu to tour Cartoon events. "We thought that there has to be authenticity and heart too when you are selling, and this is how networks opened to us," Anttu told the Swedish *Monitor Magazine* in 2021 (Dee, 2021, p. 41).

Until 2011, Cartoon Forum, EU supported pitching event for animated series, toured smaller cities across the Europe. It has been organized in Turku, Finland, in 1995, Visby, Sweden, in 2000, Kolding, Denmark, in 2005, and Stavanger, Norway, in 2009. Sopron in Western Hungary near the Austrian border had its turn in 2010. For Anttu, the Eastern European country is another home territory, as his first wife is living there with two daughters.

Finnish "Anima" had two provocative yet creative projects in "Magyar" Cartoon Forum. Petteri Pasanen, CEO of Anima Vitae at that time, presented the *Micropunks* series with Thorbjörn Jansson—a Swedish director and scriptwriter then based in Berlin. During their performance, my attention was drawn to the tanned narrow-faced guy who had chosen the best seat in the middle of the hall. He laughed out loud. Immediately after the performance, I looked to see who the Finnish–Swedish mix had brought so much joy. "I love Anima. They are my favorite studio in Europe, but far too anarchists for my channel, which is so conservative," the man snapped. I peeked at the name tag hanging on the man's chest: "Orion Ross, Disney" on the tag read.

Anttu Harlin and Eliza Jäppinen, who both worked at Anima Boutique—Anima's partner company, in those days, had the last slot on the very last day of Cartoon Forum. Anttu had dedicated to ensure that someone would stay until the last pitch. He had bought a baby bicycle from the flea market, which he swung between buildings and locked it in the prominent places. The bike was decorated with funny stickers and toys made by Eliza and her friends. The most important thing about the bike performance was that everyone detected a big note with the time and place written in capital letters when *Girls Know How and Boys Do Stuff* series project will be presented.

Both Anttu and Eliza speak English so fluently that one could think it as their mother tongue. Both have more talent in acting than the average producers or creative directors. Although they actually read the script as a dialogue, the audience began to shout at them. Not sure if Orion Ross stayed until their final presentation in Sopron event, or had already returned to his London office, as Orion himself has recalled that he was impressed by Anttu and Joonas Utti a year after.

"I first met Anttu Harlin at the time he was working in Anima. He gave a presentation at the Pictoplasma conference in Germany. After that, they developed their own product and founded the company under the same name," Ross described the encountering process in February 2021, and admitted that he has been following the creative couple since then and wanted eagerly to give them a chance to do something for Disney.

Pictoplasma is a character-driven event in Berlin, reflecting the spirit of freedom in the city, which started attracting creative people from all parts of the Europe since the Wall collapsed and the Cold War ended. Pictoplasma experimented their concept by organizing some satellite events in Amsterdam and New York; we even attempted to export the event in Finland in 2012, when Helsinki was chosen the Design Capital of the year. They said that anyone could travel to Berlin, where they could meet like-minded designers to avoid investing in a new event. The Pictoplasma style, on the other hand, has been limited to unique fantasy artworks or snowboards, which was per se a favored trend sport among many animation people in those days. Anttu's strategy was to communicate directly with organizers, while his own style preference with Joonas developed into something more classical.

Gigglebug Entertainment got started in 2013 as a pure IP studio. Then the app became very popular (Figure 5.18). In parallel with it, they had the pilot season running on *Tiny Two* (*Pikku Kakkonen*)—a magazine-type children's TV show on Yle. For an

FIGURE 5.18 *Gigglebug* was first launched as an app that became a big favorite first among Chinese kids. (With permission from Gigglebug Entertainment.)

international version, the series was done again the second time. In *Gigglebug*, the main character can get other, bad-tempered animals to laugh. The teller, familiar from classical animated series, sold the series both to mothers and grannies with a pinch of nostalgia. Watercolor backgrounds were painted on the paper with brush and pigment, and added to TV Paint and After Effects—the programs used in the beginning. Soon the company changed into Toon Boom software.

Gradually, Gigglebug reputation in broadcasting grew, and soon they were asked, "What do you have as your next project?" When the company was hired by Disney, it was the big turning point. They asked Anttu and Joonas to develop a project around "Heritage Franchise." In this case, they created a concept that was called *101 Dalmatian Street*.

Soon Gigglebug started working on another Disney project— *The Unstoppable Yellow Yeti*, which has been in development by Joonas Utti for some time. The series *The Unstoppable Yellow Yeti* is inspired by director Utti's childhood experiences. He grew up in a small town in South-Eastern Finland, and at the age of 12 the family received an exchange student from Costa Rica, who soon accelerated life in the spot. Senior pro Reid Harrison was hired to the project as a head writer (Figure 5.19).

Best and Bester project was pitched in Cartoon Forum in 2016 and gained lots of attention for a reason. It was then that the creative duo, which Harlin and Utti formed, was on everybody's lips. However, one of the successes where Gigglebug has broken through is financing. They have succeeded in applying practically every support available.

"Financing in Finland and in Nordics, more general, is actually pretty good already; you have tax credits, commissioning broadcasters, Finnish Film Foundation, Nordisk Film & TV Fond, so the progression would be to increase the funding streams that you have," says Genevieve Dexter, the London-based partner. "Perhaps more options in the broadcast arena would be good," Dexter adds.

FIGURE 5.19 The idea for *The Unstoppable Yellow Yeti* series started as a joke about yellow snow. The snow mostly turns yellow when you pee on it. There are cold, cool, and very funny moments in the series that Disney EMEA and Finnish YLE cofinanced airing on both channels since July 2022. (©With permission of Gigglebug Entertainment & Zodiak Kids Studio.)

The founder of Serious Lunch signed a coproduction deal with *Best and Bester* in 2018 and sold the series to Nickelodeon, who developed and airs it in 120 countries.

"Coming to Finland for an agreement; I had to swim in the Baltic Sea for some reason. I remember it was snowing," Dexter laughs and continues: "Commissioning broadcasters are interested in projects that are creator driven rather than pieced together by a group of entertainment executives. Having two creators who are also CEOs is not always possible, because of the wide range of skills you need to do that; so in creating a development and design studio, Gigglebug offers a unique proposition to the international community. They can draw pictures, do voice overs, and play with spreadsheets and contracts at the same time. Very unusual!"

Other key players who have worked long in Gigglebug, Anttu names Janne Korsumäki and Suvi Väkeväinen, who both came from Rovio, and Martti Sirkkola who started as an intern while still studying animation production in Tampere. Leena Lecklin, another talented storyboard artist, came from Viborg school in Denmark and has also worked in Cartoon Saloon in Kilkenny, Ireland. In the beginning of 2022, Beth Parker from Disney was appointed as the first Managing Director of the studio.

Two series, which Gigglebug studio had in production in 2022 with two different teams, are different in structure. *Best & Bester* is a modern tale where characters can transform their bodies into something different, change their conditions. The idea is to highlight that there are always many opinions, and diversity gets celebrated. In *Yeti,* the story revolves around friendship and rebelling against rules that the newcomer can confront, but friends are having fun too.

Learning curve for a small Finnish startup is steep. In *101 Dalmatian Street,* the lead studio status went to Passion Animation Studios in London, which was a disappointment though understandable. Animation production was done in Atomic Cartoons in Vancouver, Canada. In Gigglebug, the studio there were made funny shorts like Christmas presents for the smallest puppies published on YouTube.

"Step by step you progress. We love this industry and believe that spreading joy has a meaning. It is fun, and doing animations and creating, in general, is fun," says the CEO, who is also a frequents speaker in many industry events from Cartoon Business to Kidscreen Summit, referring in those talks to the country of Bhutan, which introduced Gross Nation Happiness indicator instead of Gross Domestic Product.

Anttu claims that Nordic animation is driven by values. From Finland, he praises the school system, which is very holistic in nature: "If Gigglebug's focus is in laughter and spreading joy, being positive can help anyone. In pedagogy, it means that rather than teaching which trees by their biologic terms are growing in the forest, you encourage a child to enter the forest with an open mind and experience new things."

CLOSING THE CIRCLE—*TITINA*

The first, just one-minute-long animation in Norway was made by Sverre Halvorsen (1891–1936) in 1913 on Roald Amundsen's travel to South Pole (*Roald Amundsen på sydpolen*). During the time of writing this book, one of the most ambitious Nordic feature projects *Titina* was finishing its production in Norway and Belgium (Figure 5.20).

The new light, mostly bright and solid colored, feature takes viewers on a trip to the North Pole with Roald Amundsen and a small terrier, who was rescued by his cotraveller, Italian Umberto Nobile to wander around the streets of Rome. After more than 25 years of making shorts, Norwegian studio Mikrofilm, awarded once with an Oscar and nominated twice for their shorts, is finally making an animated feature with the concept that is born under the lucky stars, accidentally closing the circle—the North circle.

"Getting an Oscar in 2007 was a miracle to Mikrofilm," recalls CEO and producer Lise Fearnley (b. 1969). "We actually had limited business at that time of making *The Danish Poet* in 2006. Director Torill Kove (b. 1958), of course, had high ambitions, but you need a lot of luck in winning an Oscar; and, on the other hand, luck is not enough. The win gave us new spark; it was really encouraging. Although there was a lot of collaboration with other companies and National Film Board of Canada as a financing partner, the fact that Mikrofilm was a major producer of that film is very important to us," she concludes.

Kove's first film, an 11-minute short *My Grandmother Ironed the King's Shirts* (1999) was also nominated, but Mikrofilm has just been founded that time. Instead, the short was produced by Studio Magica—an influential stop-motion company of the 1990s of which most successful shorts were directed by Russian-born Pjotr Sapegin featuring a character called Edvard, loosely based on the life of the Norwegian composer Edvard Grieg, and *One Day a Man Bought a House* (*Huset på Kampen*, 1998), which won a lot of awards, including Hiroshima.

FIGURE 5.20   Colonel Umberto Nobile had his terrier Titina with all expeditions he made with airship Italia. (©Italian Air Force Museum of Vigna di Valle, With permission from Mikrofilm.)

Another film by Torill Kove *Me and My Moulton* (2014) was nominated in 2015. Traveling with Torill's film to many festivals, from Toronto to Berlin, was very interesting, both for the director, who has settled in Canada, and the producer who kept long devoted for shorts due to the financing schemes available at Norwegian Film Institute.

"Financing animated series in Norway is not easy. NRK—the public broadcasting company is not interested in investing in national productions; they rather buy something cheaper from overseas. Features are very commercial, but in shorts there is more artistic freedom," says Tonje Skar Reiersen b. (1979), who was hired by Mikrofilm at the time Torill Kove was directing *Hocus Pocus Alfie Atkins* (2013)—a Danish–Swedish–Norwegian feature in Maipo Film.

Both Tonje and Lise think that Norway and its neighboring Nordic countries have been lacking a big TV series. One Norwegian example that got quite close is *Elias: The Little Rescue Boat* (2005–2008). "It is very well made," says Lise. "We had many ideas for series in the past too, but it was impossible to finance them. You have to convince the broadcaster from the beginning. On NRK they are focusing strongly on Norwegian kids appearing in their series, and animation has not that strict nationality."

Tonje has her background in film and media studies, she has worked as a film critic and in film festivals, while Lise used to study photography. Lise and Kajsa Næss (b. 1970), her cofounder and a director for the first feature *Titina* (2022), met as both were students at Oslo Film & TV Academy.

Their graduation film was a stop-motion animated short *Toothsome* (*Pussig*). It received already many prizes. I was present when the other early *Skummelt* (*Ragged*) won a special prize at the first Nordic Glory festival in Jyväskylä, Finland. The festival founded in 1997 was one of the first attempts to highlight women in film and media arts long before #metoo movement.

"At Mikrofilm both the management and owners are women, but also having an art collective attitude was important to us," Lise explains.

In 1996, when Mikrofilm was established together with Lise Fearnley, Kajsa Næss, and also a third partner Liv Berit Helland, their first animated film *Mother Said* (*Sa mor*, 1998) used the animation technique photopixillation—a variant of stop-motion, where still images are used as "dolls." A bit different method, polaroid images pressed on to watercolor paper was in use when Næss and Mikkel Brænne Sandemose made a music video for the song *Abigail* by Bertine Zetliz (Parker, 2020).

Lise tells that first films at Mikrofilm were shot on 16 mm camera, and you have to know the camera well; thus, she benefited from the background as a photographer. "I did an internship in newspaper, and the work was not what I expected. I quitted, and went on directing and developing films."

Visual emphasis has remained strong in the company ever since and also the quality of film-making to every detail. A couple of years ago, Mikrofilm was asked to do an immersive film project to a major art museum. "It was about filling the room with living paintings by Edvard Munch. I think, it was not a good idea. His compositions are nice but characters are not easily animated."

The transition from shorts to the first feature is also about times that are just different. "Now there is a boom for content, and Nordic content sells equally to any other content."

Lise believes in scalable productions: A short can also end up into a series or a feature format. At Mikrofilm, they have been fortunate that shorts can pay a producer, a director, and a whole team. If there were 13 animators working for *The Danish Poet*, the number of employees has been increasing. "We do not have a huge talent pool of classical 2D animators yet in Norway yet. It will probably take some time until it gets better, as there are good graduates coming from Volda or from Viborg, which is one of the best schools in Europe. However, the best 2D school is in Bournemouth University," Lise knows.

Titina is an ambitious arthouse film with 8,000,000 Euro budget. Fifty five percent of that comes from Norway and the rest from Belgium. Spending Norwegian money overseas is possible, but you have to be clever with the financing.

The idea came from Kajsa. Roald Amundsen is a big hero in Norway, but the story the film bases is not very well known. Both Amundsen and Italian Nobile, who had a dog Titina always with him, made many trips to the North Pole. The first expedition was in 1926. In 1928, Nobile went there without Amundsen. But search parties from many countries went looking for them when they crashed, including Amundsen. And this is when Amundsen disappeared (Figure 5.21).

Parts of the wreck were found but not any bodies. In all, 17 lives were wasted, and Nobile was so disgraced that he went into exile. Not only everyone died in the crash with Airship Italia, but also people died searching for Italia, including Amundsen and his crew.

FIGURE 5.21 *Titina* (2022) bases on a true story with the expedition by Norwegian and Italian teams over the North Pole told from the perspective of a dog. (With permission from Mikrofilm/Vivi Film.)

"The story is seen through the eyes of Nobile's dog who was on both the expeditions. There are scenes inspired by magical realism—a freedom only animation can offer. We are also developing two other feature films," Tonje confirms.

The Belgian could offer their experience with classical 2D that was needed to achieve the desired quality in the production. A lead character designer comes from Norway with a background as a newspaper cartoonist. Unique coloring is made so that air is so crisp that you can feel it. Distribution is in hands of the French sales agent Les Films du Losange, with many strong art house titles in its portfolio.

"We think in Norway it is easy to make this film big, get as big audience as possible," Lise says. There will be a book and other marketing stuff. "The film has a broad appeal. It is a family film with a lot of humor, not a history lesson. There will be some moments that are larger than life, even surrealistic sequences. And it is not necessary that characters are already popular; we are making new heroes," Lise adds.

Considering the situation of how animation industry can grow in Nordics, financing is another big issue along restrictions with a Nordic talent pool delayed by unefficiency at some schools. In addition to her work in Mikrofilm, Tonje has been a driving force in defining and operating actions of a Nordic Animation network in Mifa and other European animation events since 2018. "The aim of Nordic Animation collective is to promote own products and to become more attractive as coproducers. Another important goal is to strengthen cooperation between Nordic producers and have a stronger profile internationally," Tonje listed in an article for the Swedish *Monitor Magazine* in 2021 (Dee, 2021, p. 36).

"Another challenge is to increase national support in each country. In the individual countries, producers are now working strategically to improve funding, and it is at this point that it is important to be able to refer to the brand that Nordic Animation has established."

FIGURE 5.22 In her opening speech for Nordic Spotlight at Cartoon Movie 2022, Tonje Skar Reiersen said that Nordic original stories speak what it means to be human. "Stories with characters that challenge our expectations make us see the world and ourselves in a new light, showing that people are equal, no matter how different". (Courtesy of Cartoon.)

For the question, if Nordic countries are seen bundled in the Anglo-Saxon world, Tonje sees that as discussed within the network it is actually ok. "It is not so dangerous if people abroad do not know that Astrid Lindgren is Swedish or that there are no mountains in Denmark. The important thing is that they begin to connect the Nordic countries and Nordic animation with quality, innovation, transparency, cost-effectiveness, and animation for children—a solid tradition. While American and French animated films usually focus on the individual, Nordic stories are often about what we can do together. We do not talk so much about the differences between us; rather, we focus on what we have in common," Tonje concludes (Figure 5.22).

Epilogue

TROLLS AND MORE TROLLS

If traditional trolls are mostly considered slow-witted and ugly, why bother making them alive in animation. One could think that cute and witty kids, or cute and witty animals, are an easier way to make a profit. In conclusion, I intend to prove that the more sophisticated characters are, the more successful they are in variations and licensing. Media sales are not a great source of revenue in the current world with the harsh competition; money is made with collateral merchandise. Therefore, repetition and a clear concept are also necessary.

What does sophistication in animation mean? This came up in the conversation with Eric Shaw Scot—one of the scriptwriters for *SpongeBob* and *Puppet Babies*. He was facilitating a workshop with Finnish animation professionals in 2016 and gave a lecture on his experiences in consulting the growing Chinese animation industry. Shaw said that Chinese animation could never become quite as successful as animation from Japan, because China lacks sophistication as a culture. Many have said the same thing about Russian culture. Both Chinese and Russian appeal to the glitzy kitsch rather than simplistic yet functional forms is possibly reflecting the era where both the societies or at least a part of it were growing economically; but it has not always been like that.

I have found fantastic Soviet animation in the Finnish film archive made until the 1960s, and I have heard that the Indian animation talent inherits from the tuition of the Moscow film school.

I have also found Chinese art very sophisticated, from traditional vertical paintings to installations with the most surprising materials. Yet, having been to Las Vegas or Orlando, the American kitsch heavens, one might long for tranquility of the temples found just around the corner in Asia, including the Japanese islands and the megalomaniac superpower China.

Comparing Japanese and Chinese cultures is not fair, though they have many similarities. I have been told that Chinese monks took the Chinese culture, from Chinese characters to ink painting, to the islands of Japan. The sophistication of Japanese anime was developed within an elaborated, disciplined, and using a challenging format, before the digital era with computers. Where studio Ghibli, with masters like Hayao Miyazaki, introduced anime to the world, younger directors are now copying this style, but with less sophistication. Nevertheless, in general, the Japanese cultural landscape is so crowded with characters from anime and manga, or their lookalikes, that it is hard to find any other culture to compete with it. Not even the Belgium capital Brussels or the French city of Angoulême can give you the same overwhelming feeling of living the life of a cartoon character, here and now. No Nordic nation has yet achieved this level although we have our Moominland and other theme parks.

Before the invasion of the characterization, Japanese design was nearly as low-key as in the Nordics, with the dominance of black color, adjacent to white or nude, pure forms with no decoration, and complete absence of glitter. One might think that the Japanese preference for Scandinavian and Finnish design lies in their likeness to Japanese, but it can be quite the opposite as well. The minimalism of Iittala, formerly Arabia, tableware designed in the late 1940s is very Japanese to my eye too. Japonism as a movement among European artists in the late 1800s took influence directly from Japan (Figure 6.1). Light tones with soft lining used in Japanese decoration is familiar to the generation of my grandma from the children's books, illustrations, and greeting cards they had.

Identifying a typical Finnish old building is impossible. All the houses reference the Nordic cottage style or later influences of the

FIGURE 6.1 Lithuanian artist M.K. Čiurlionis belongs to the artists in Northern Europe who have been influenced by Japanese art. Their style has also been called Japonism. *Sonata No.5 (Sonata of the Sea) Finale* is from 1908. Tempera on paper 73.2×63. (Courtesy of M.K. Čiurlionis Nationl Museum of Art, Lithuania, Čt14.)

Russian era, namely the adaptation of the Empire style—a form of recycled neoclassism. The further east you travel in Russia, the more decorative the houses get, borrowing in style from folk art rather than from the palaces of emperors. Is it this aesthetics from magnificent palaces that distinguishes sophistication? No.

One could also argue that art nouveau developed too kitschy in England, with Crystal Palace. The Great Exhibition in 1851 was a chock with industrially manufactured items having no style and no sophistication.

Art nouveau is nowadays admired in Finnish and Latvian capitals as original, local, and one of the most typical styles. There was a time when it was considered too decorative. There have always been attempts to hide the lousy decoration suddenly turned unpopular by the changes in political hegemony. Thus, the concept of sophistication changes. Gnarl furniture might be seen as something most ugly, no matter whether made in Finnish North Ostrobothnia or China. When the material sense of authenticity disappears, it makes little matter what the thing looks like. In CGI (Computer Generated Imagery) animation, the look and feel of plastic goes fine. A worldwide audience has very little connection with authentic materials like wood or wool. Some might say that making the sense of material visible addressees the question of quality in animation better than the stupid question of "2D or 3D." In 2D, the reference point could be illustrations, and it were caricatures at the pioneer era, not so much material.

Giving a new tool, like a lathe, into the hands of the inexperienced woodworker produces ugly furniture or tableware with no respect to the wood as a material with own features. Instead, when the causes of a tree are left visible, and the forms given by the tool align them, we think this is in good taste, because we respect nature as such. On the other hand, when the respect for nature disappears, and no reference is not even longed for by anyone, we step in a world of peril.

Digital tools can also be insidious. For example, artists who have pioneered with software like Photoshop or Maya can easily be criticized for overusing a particular feature. This gives the impression that they do not know how to use the tool; they make the tool a subject, instead of their art.

Different variants show how vital the animation character has become; it also opens licensing opportunities and turns the creations into cash. The best Nordic case of this is the Moomins. The offspring of Tove Jansson's two brothers have done their best in doing so, although Tove too modified the characters already, herself, for many uses in her lifetime.

Many Norwegian, Danish, and Swedish animators have been influenced by John Bauer's trolls, and so was Finnish Tove Jansson. I am wondering which other yet unexploited mythological characters could be turned to successful products. An example of this, if not that ancient history, is bringing to life the legendary character of Titina, from the film *Titina*, making the real-life terrier hound of Roald Amundsen a famous character in the animated feature premiered in fall 2022.

Stepping a bit outside animation, Norwegian artist Tori Wrånes makes interesting rapprochement with trolls. Partly sculptures in a gallery and partly performances in surprising locations, she has shaken contemporary conception of reality. Her creatures have been called Hobbits and Ewoks, depending on which popular films, from *Lord of the Rings* to *Star Wars*, the spectator is familiar with. Her performance on the last day of the Thailand Biennale in 2018 was assisted by the Polish animator Monika Lyko who told me the story. The performance was recorded by an American journalist canoeing with his friends through Krabi archipelago. When the video went viral, people took for granted that there must be an unknown relative to humans—a species or beings living in the caves. It produced more than 30,000 views in a short course of time and many astonished comments.

The artist named the project *Closest Relatives*. She says she does not represent a troll as a romantic national figure but rather as a character symbolizing the unregulated—a creature that deviates from the norm and makes up its own, alternative rules. The approach is close to that of the award-winning Swedish film *Border* (Gräns 2018), where the troll made an entrance as a customs worker with an ability to smell the fear. If animation as a form of expression no longer does convey the questions of reality, and if it goes beyond the most apparent domains and further away from its original points of reference, how it survives as an art form, or are we losing it for business? This might not need to happen in such a way.

THE AUTHOR'S FINAL WORD

I am from Finland, where people are the happiest in the world according to the World Happiness Report, but I was born as a miserable child just like Greta Thunberg and an angry young adult. There was not much wrong with our school system, our healthcare was close to perfect with multiple vaccination programs, but I felt sad for the rest of the world which has later opened to me in the most generous ways.

Art Education was my major at the university, not Animation. I was angry at my university rector Aino Sallinen, who started her tenure in 1992. I interviewed her when the depression hit Finnish media industry in 1992. The Soviet Union collapsed, and left my kind of visually orientated journalists unemployed. The professor of journalism has also made me feel angry, and I can blame him for leaving for London, where I took some animation courses, because it was something I loved the most. I was also angry at my professor in Finland who has said animation is the only media thing that is never made in Finland. I wanted to prove that he was wrong. The world has changed a lot from those days, and it is changing rapidly all the time.

Poorly educated in England lacking computer-literate teachers, I did not become an animator myself. In the early 1990s, British animators used computers only for testing animation but not for making animation. Instead, I have promoted Finnish animation since 2009 and initiated the Nordic collaboration since 2016. It was the mission after the Asia Strategy that I was leading in Finnanimation. Hope this explains my approach that is neither historical nor technical but personal and having the Asia perspective along the Western world, meaning Western Europe and North America.

When I got a job with Finnanimation—the network of Finnish animation producers promoting Finnish animation, it was because

I had done marketing communications. I did not have my background in film, neither as a producer, director, or animator. Producers who hired me had already started branding "Finnish animation" under Finnanimation. When there were younger people like Anttu Harlin joining the network a bit later, and they started to refer to "Nordic Animation" as a value-driven genre, or Nordic Joy most recently, I greeted the Nordic as a value very positive. Personally, I have come to the term "Nordic Animation," since traveling so much in Asia. In global perspective we are united.

In this book, I have avoided writing about Finnish, Danish, Norwegian, Icelandic, or Swedish animation. I rather write about Nordic Animation.

When you talk about the larger region, there are the same conditions and the same values that are shared, rather than any nationalistic ideals. The latter ones can also be negative. In the global world, Nordic ideals on the contrary are something that can be both admired and also copied as a larger principle, although the financing models still remain mostly nationalistic (Figure 6.2) national, and in commercial formats such as film or tv series, animation is very commercial depending on the financing.

Let's compare Scandinavia to Shanghai for a moment. Shanghai had the World Expo in 2010, and all the Scandinavian pavilions stood there on the row with bright and shiny white walls, and brilliant Scandinavian design displayed next to the latest achievements of digital telecommunications. I had just started working with the Finnish animation producers' association and traveled there with three producers: Jim Solatie who has been making the Finnish-originating *Dibidogs* series in the Guangzhou province, making it one of the first Chinese–Finnish co-productions; Tom Carpelan who was about to launch new animated features from old stop-motion Moomins; and Petteri Pasanen, whose company in those days Anima Vitae did *The Daily Ape Show* in order to entertain the Chinese taxi passengers with the facts about Finland. Later, the taxi shorts were developed into the TV series that run on YLE for one-and-half seasons with 17 episodes (Figure 6.3).

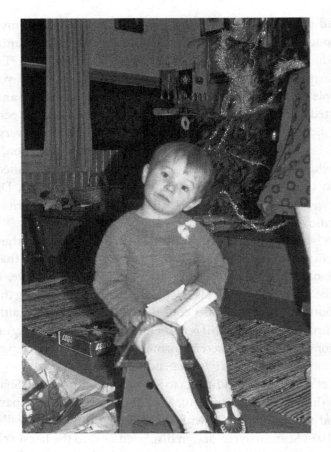

FIGURE 6.2 Favorite presents for every Nordic child would be LEGO Systems, books by Nordic authors, pens and pencils, and notebooks to create your own art. Television came into our home in 1969, but there was nothing interesting to watch for a 3 year old. (Image provided by the author.)

What I learned in Shanghai Expo is that there are no better countries in the world than five Nordic states or just a few. You can spot us from the world map, even the population of Shanghai exceeds the five countries. One city is just more enormous, and

FIGURE 6.3 *The Daily Ape Show* screened in Finland Pavilion at Shanghai Expo in 2010. (Image provided by the author.)

how many of these megalopolises are there in China or the rest of Asia. And do we even know their names? Asia has a lesson in the world market, which we all need to study a bit. I have been learning it intensively since 2010, with many trips to China, Hong Kong, South Korea, Japan, Malaysia, Thailand, and India. I could also say that if Finns have been welcomed to join the rest of Scandinavians, because we are not actually part of Scandinavia when it is referred to as a geographical term, and our language is so different compared to languages spoken in Sweden, Norway, Iceland, and Denmark, which precisely makes us the happiest people in the world.

Appendix A

NOMAD STORIES: Virpi Kettu in the UK and Canada

Virpi Kettu (b. 1975) is Finland's first animated celebrity and an animation nomad who has lived in nine countries. Sharp-sighted Finnish journalists spotted her name from the credits of the *Wallace & Gromit* animations in mid-2000s. Born in Ilomantsi near the Russian border, Kettu has been interviewed in Finnish and international newspapers also, because she made music videos for the cult band Radiohead from Oxford and superstar Katy Perry from the USA (Figure A.1).

A few journalists, including myself, started to take an interest in the new British animations because of MTV's inventive channel IDs. Aardman's clay animations were another favorite of that time; and many wondered how a Finn had ended up making them at the time there was only one animation school in Finland.

Animation has been taught since the 1970s in the Helsinki College of Art and Design, now Aalto University, but mostly for students majoring in Art Education, Graphic Arts, or Stage Design. In Turku, the first full-time animation school started in 1994.

FIGURE A.1 Finnish Virpi Kettu was working in Aardman Animations in the early 2000s when Finnish animation industry was taking its first steps. (With permission from Virpi Kettu.)

Kettu started her studies in Turku in 1995, but she could not apply in the animation course; in the beginning they only took students to that class every third year. Therefore, Kettu chose to study Visual Arts as her major. Turku Arts Academy has a long-going tradition to be a drawing school thus giving a good technical foundation that helped her in animation that she studied for 1 year at Diagonal Academy in Visby in Gotland, Sweden.

Kettu had only been to the Swedish animation school for the first year when she heard from industry people visiting the school that there is a possibility to do an internship at Aardman in Bristol, UK. The 6-month internship was supported by the Swedish state fund. While modeling the world's best clay animation in Bristol as a Swedish student, Kettu neither did meet other Finns nor Swedes. Several Danes had ended up with Aardman, most of them graduates from Viborg's Animation Workshop. An Icelandic cameraman also worked in the studio, and Kettu became good friends with him too.

Swedish schoolmates did not follow Kettu's example, as most of them found work in Trollhättan, where animation and film production was set up in the former Saab factories with regional funding from Film I Väst.

Kettu didn't have to feel homesick though. "I didn't consider myself a foreigner, because the animation communities are international families." On the other hand, she had a bit of a gloomy picture of Finland in those days. "Sweden is a society where there used to be more support for a wide range of creative activities. Finland, on the other hand, has developed more recently as an art nation, and arts have only begun to be valued over the last 20 years," Kettu recalls the times of her exile. "In my own family, art could not be a career choice. Animation was not appreciated even in Turku in early years," Kettu reminiscents.

The first period in England lasted 7 years. In between, Kettu went to animate the popular *Pingu* series in Manchester. At Aardman, she got involved in both series and feature productions. The big incident was *Creature Comforts* comedy taking place in the zoo. The short film version had already brought the first Oscar to the company in Bristol in 1990. Director Nick Park has amassed his entire 1990s award cabinet not only with the Oscars but also with the BAFTA awards for two shorter and one long *Wallace and Gromit* films where Kettu was also animating with a couple of hundred colleagues.

Despite her enjoyment in Bristol, the North Karelian nomad decided to move next to Canada. Canada's reputation in animation has grown year by year, thanks to the generous state support and an influential neighbor. Kettu also had a Canadian animation idol, and she followed him to North America. "Aardman looked good on my CV, I guess, and it was easy to get involved with the local projects," says Virpi. In Toronto, she worked for the longest time at the Cuppa Coffee Studio, which has trained many Canadian animation professionals.

Kettu understands well why Rovio and other success stories are important to Finns. On the contrary, in Toronto, there was all the time a lot of work available for animation professionals. At times,

Kettu moved to Montreal and even applied for Canadian citizenship feeling happy with the high work ethics. "The fan hum just started to piss me off one hot summer day. I felt being a tiny part of the big factory who has been animating the same character for a months," Kettu says.

Kettu says that thanks to digitalization and the internet, she may as well live in a small town in the north of England with a medieval castle in the middle and wool mills reminiscent of the early days of industrialization. After 9 years in Canada, Virpi Kettu decided to move back to England but not to Bristol any more. Livestock has been transported along the canals to the nearest big city, Leeds.

Many of the factories and mills have since the old days been turned into museums or spacious loft apartments. Traditional stone houses are cold, the wind blowing through them, but an even colder ride has been brought to the community not only by Brexit but also by a severe pandemic. Kettu was shocked by the inequality in British society and became active in the Labour Party: "England is a rich country where things could be much better." She wants to take responsibility for her surroundings and make stories about the Yorkshire Dales in her home village.

"If New York is a legendary city, it's just because great stories are told about it," Kettu says. Some of her animations are political. "It would feel like a great success if I could help people to understand how much power over their own lives they actually have and how lives could be made better just by knowing basic civic information. The media is able to lie because they are big monopolies. The world needs visualizations right now about how things work in this world as well as how the world can be saved." According to Kettu, British education needs to change. Brexit has given birth to new uncertainty among students about where and how their degrees are valid.

Kettu teaches animation in many colleges and universities. With her students, she has often pondered the concept of success. "Animation is a difficult field where self-torture is not avoided. Production requires and, on the other hand, teaches patience. Doing it alone does not go far, but a team is sought for every production. Finding a working group is already a big part of success," Kettu assures.

Although an animator has to learn a new computer program every 6 months, pure nerds don't succeed in the business, nor do those who just concentrate on the art. The industry needs and likes a multitasker. Kettu has received local and regional support for making her own *Dogs Dale* stories. In addition, she has set up a charity network, Carven Arts, for local artists providing studio buildings where artists can exhibit and work affordably. In addition, the location hosts art events and various workshops. Kettu has been lucky in many ways and wants to give back to her community: "The hatred towards immigrants has felt bad, because I am one of them too. Dealing with propagandist anger is important. It is difficult to eradicate misinformation, but I think education with animation and gamification as a part of it can be a great tool in the fight for a better society" (Figure A.2).

FIGURE A.2   Virpi Kettu hesitates to call herself an artist and prefers to be titled as a professional in the creative industry. She works mostly with plasticine but learns a new computer program every half a year. (With permission from Virpi Kettu.)

Appendix B

NOMAD YEARS: Rölli in Russia and Lisa Limone in Estonia

Whereas some Russian and Polish animators have settled in Norway to influence its industry and Danish A. Film, some Finns have braved enough to try Russian Cooperation. Marko Röhr—the producer of the *Rölli-Quest for a Heart* feature—has said that when he was presenting his film project with a popular character in Turku Arts Academy, animation students were not interested working in it. Partly for that reason the film was made in Moscow. Thus, art director Janne Kopu became the first Finnish animation nomad to travel East.

Kopu as well as producer Röhr were both fans of traditional drawn animation, so 3D studio Anima Vitae was not an option for their project. It was directed by Pekka Lehtosaari, who has experienced in dubbing Disney films in Finnish. The director also had to settle in Moscow.

One film project in Russia was enough for the producer though. "It was completely impossible to sell the film in Western European countries," Röhr has said in an interview I conducted in 2010. The brand performed moderately well in the local licensing market. Rölli Easter eggs were sold for years, and the character also won the 'Satusuomalainen', meaning Fairytale Finn, vote organized by YLE. Röll's first animated film had its merits.

Compared to Moscow, which has many animation studios, or St. Petersburg, which has less but a few big ones, Tallinn is relatively a big animation destination with two amazing animation studios that have both survived well the Soviet years. Nukufilm is one of my favorite studios in the world, and I have toured them quite a lot. It has been in operation since 1957 and been located in a church enabling tremendous camera rides over their sets. For Finnish animation professionals, precisely, and also for other Nordic nationals, Nukufilm has offered service work. The unique studio also creates its own IPs receiving special subsidies with Nukufilm add-ons.

The other Soviet survivor and still-operating studio is Joonisfilm, which split from Tallinnafilm in 1971. It makes classical drawn animations, while Nukufilm is a puppet animation studio.

A number of Finnish students from the Turku Arts Academy (Figure B.1) have become acquainted with Finland's southern neighbor during the internship making *Lisa Limone and Maroc Orange: A Rapid Love Story* (2013). They made city scenes and stuffed tomato fields and ketchup jars in a rare stop-motion feature, discussing the refugee problem well before its bleakest years.

"Time stops at Nukufilm studio. The atmosphere is somehow sacred when everyone is kind of busy and fussing around, and next staying deeply concentrated in their own corner without talking to no one," Kati Kovács, the creator of Lisa Limone and Marco Orange characters, describes.

It was a true coincidence that the Finnish-born but Rome-based cartoonist Kati Kovács and Tallinn's Nukufilm began to collaborate in 2006. Kovács held two joint exhibitions with another Finnish cartoonist Timo Mäkelä in Estonia—one in Tallinn and the other in Tartu. The photographer who worked at the time for

FIGURE B.1   Sanni Lahtinen and Joni Männistö enjoying the night by Annecy Lake in 2011 when Finnish producers organized a sauna party for the second time. (Image provided by the author.)

Postimees magazine and also at Nukufilm was following their work and taking pictures from both exhibitions, and they got to know each other pretty well. After some good talks over one pint and another, Kovács was asked to write a screenplay, as Nukufilm was looking for something new. For a small country, foreign talent is not turned back.

Without any grants or script studies in long-format drama, a synopsis started developing along some early sketches of characters. Finally, a full script was handed over to Estonians in October 2006. As soon as December 2006, the Finnish comic artist received a positive response from a Tallinn studio, and the contract was signed (Figure B.2).

After 1 year from delivering the rights from Kovács to Nukufilm, the young director Mait Laas announced his desire

FIGURE B.2   Cartoonist Kati Kovács found her folder with first sketches for Lisa Limone and Maroc Orange—the main characters for her 2013 feature film. (Image provided by the author.)

to direct The Love Story of Lisa Limone and Maroc Orange. Lait wanted to make it like a soap opera, and because opera songs can be performed in their original languages, the studio attempted to avoid dubbing into different language versions. A typical Estonian budget could give that no allowance. Eventually, there are four languages in the film, as some songs are sung in Italian, some in French, and some in English. In the end also Estonian is spoken.

International sales agents were horrified by the multilingual solution. No surprise, the film has not been sold for theatrical distribution in any country. With the exception of festival performances, there has been very little opportunity to see an exceptional film. At the Tallinn premiere in the autumn of 2013, absolutely everyone, including Finnish coproducers from Bufo, its Finnish production company, was present, and it is said to be a good party for 2 days.

I heard about the film for the first time when I was registering as a member of the press at the Stuttgart Festival of Animated Film in April 2014. My pre-expectations were not particularly high, because advance information I had received stated that there is no Finnish animation in the program, although the centennial of Finnish animation was celebrated the same year.

"There is one Finnish feature film here," I was corrected at the press registration desk. Since I was listening to Mait's personal presentation of the film, I had been a big fan of his work, and Nukufilm in general, in addition to Kovács's art.

Obviously, the production took a long time to complete, about 7 years (I have heard about longer production times too with some French arthouse animations), and sometimes the creator Kati Kovács, better known as a cartoonist, thought too that it would never be completed. The idea in the beginning was to make the film only half-an-hour long, but it was stretched to 72 minutes, rarely a good idea. However, at this time, extra support was obtained from Finland, and, in the end, according to the director, Finland was its biggest financier, bigger than Estonia. However, the Finnish Film Foundation, YLE, or the Finnish film production company had sadly no interest in marketing the film completed in November 2013.

Extending a short format concept into a feature length brings seldom a good result, although that is often done to please one or two financiers, but the execution of *Lisa Limone and Maroc Orange: A Rapid Love Story* is not bad at all; rather, it is both funny and very imaginative. Most of all, it can be seen as the handcraft of director Mait Laas, who is very much a nature child like some of us in Nordics are. Moreover, the refugee issue has become a shocking topic throughout Europe but could be made rather in an animated documentary than in a scatty love story. In those days *Waltz with Bazhir* has not yet won its Oscars to start the boom very popular in Denmark and Norway later on.

The rare film tells the story of African refugees landing in Sicily, many of whom are unfortunate. In the story written by Kovács, Maroc and his friends are saved and hired as tomato pickers. "I wanted to make an international story, not a Finnish one. Italy is the first country to receive refugees from the south, but the problem affects all of us," Kovács explains (Figure B.3).

The Estonian feature has remained so far her only effort in the film business, but in comics Kovács is very productive and admired as a hero for a generation of female comics, those influencing also the new generation of female animators (Figure B.4).

FIGURE B.3 Finnish–Estonian coproduction *Lisa Limone and Maroc Orange: A Rapid Love Story* (2013) tells about the European refugee problem. (With permission from ©Nukufilm 2013 by Ragnar Neljandi.)

FIGURE B.4 The happy ending of *Lisa Limone and Maroc Orange: A Rapid Love Story* made in Tallinn, Estonia. (With permission of ©Nukufilm 2013 by Ragnar Neljandi.)

Appendix C

NOMAD STORIES: Veronica Wallenberg – a cosmopolitan

Swedish Veronica Wallenberg is a true animation nomad. Veronica has been working both as a lead 2D animator and a director in many cities from Stockholm to Antarctica. She cannot say how many countries she has actually worked from, but she has been to all the continents.

When she lived in Berlin, she noticed that TED conferences were looking for an animator. So she applied to be one of them. It was around 2012, she signed a contract to do a dozen films. Because of this, she decided to make one film in one place, starting with the US, and then she continued around the globe.

After making the first film *The Survival of the Sea Turtle* (2012), she took a holiday in Indonesia volunteering in a sea turtles rescue.

I have probably met Veronica for the first time in Annecy, where she seemed to be very much socializing with everyone. That was the time Finnanimation was organizing hugely popular tent sauna parties by the lake.

Once when Veronica was visiting Finland, we had a meeting point near the underground station in Hakaniemi market square

(Hagnäs in Swedish). I was surprised how many people she has arranged to meet on the same go. Carrying their backpacks, they had just a stop-over in Helsinki, but she was active enough to meet with many friends she has made in the Finnish animation scene.

Veronica started her studies in 3D animation studies at Stockholm university, but she did not like it. "The level was just too low, so I dropped out voluntarily," Veronica says.

"Education does not matter as much as a portfolio, at least not in Sweden. Maybe, if you've been to Viborg in Denmark or Gobelins in France or to an animation school in the USA, your school matters on your CV. I have mostly learned by doing."

Studios where she has worked for in Sweden include Dockhus in Trollhättan, where she only jumped in, and Filmtecknarna in Stockholm, where she was happy to belong to the group of eight animators who did animated scenes for the Academy award-winning film *Searching for a Sugar Man* (2012).

After Filmtecknarna she has also been working with LEE Film both in productions *Gordon & Paddy* and *The Ape Star* directed by Linda Hambäck. "It was like working as a family, very cozy atmosphere," Veronica tells.

She thinks that one of her most notable animation projects is the 1-minute film *Stink-a-boo* (2019) about passive smoking. When WHO (World Health Organization) picked it up in 2020 for their website, it became hugely popular. It was done by Cinematic—an animation studio Veronica founded in Stockholm in 2007 together with Johan Sonestedt.

Motivated to work collaboratively, both Johan and Veronica put together teams for interesting 2D projects both for adults and kids, direct, supervise, animated, and provided comp. Cinematic has also been organizing the monthly reoccurring networking event—The Animationbar in Stockholm.

Other notable shorts by Cinematic include *Vox Lipoma* (*Fettknölen*, 2018), which was selected for Sundance Film Festival and nominated for Short Film Grand Jury Prize. Its script is made by Jane Magnusson and Liv Strömqvist. The film was funded by the Swedish Film Institute, Film Stockholm, and SVT. And the short was partially celebrating the 100 years' anniversary of Sweden's most legendary film director Ingmar Bergman questioning his importance by having fun with his sexual obsessions.

"Denmark and Norway have lots of talent in making good feature films and animated documentaries, Sweden is more focused on games, and the sector keeps growing. Many animation studios are doing cinematics, game trailers, or advertising. We are helping each other out. Veronica adds"

Veronica likes hand-drawn 2D, and she thinks it's sad that not more people in Sweden go in that direction instead of VFX, games, and 3D. The advertising sector has very good companies like Brikk that creates game trailers, commercials, social media campaigns, title sequences, online videos, infomercials, and web animations on their reference list. A lot of companies are not very keen on developing their own IP. It's easier to make money on the commercial side.

Veronica names Finnish Rovio an opposite example in how it has expanded to other areas than just games. Her business partner Johan works remotely for Finnish Rovio. To be nominated as the coolest brand in Nordics, Veronica picks up the studio Gigglebug, which is very energetic, and making her smile: "I love the style they've managed to develop" (Figure C.1).

FIGURE C.1 Veronica Wallenberg has been working in all the continents. In Sweden, she was animating *Gordon and Paddy* for LEE Film. (With permission from Cinematic.)

Appendix D

NOMAD YEARS: Antonia Ringbom and "Tjejmafian"

Before the 21st century, Finnish animation artists became international, mostly in connection with their Nordic colleagues. As the language of cooperation was Swedish or Scandinavian, Finnish–Swedes, such as Antonia Ringbom (b. 1946), benefited from the cooperation. The Finnish director got Golden Gunnar Life Time Achievement Award in Stockholm, Sweden in 2014 (Figure D.1).

After her retirement from running cultural activities in the city of Hanko (Hangö in Swedish), Ringbom moved to Korppoo in the archipelago (Korpo in Swedish), where she has a tiny animation studio built of clay and straw, and continues animating her identifiable cut-out animations in all bright colors.

Every winter, Ringbom takes off to Africa, where her *Yellow Giraffe's Animal Stories* (1997) got inspiration from—the series 26×7 produced by Mikael Wahlforss at Epidem ZOT production company. It received the UNICEF prize and Silver Pulcinella for the Best Series in Europe in 1997. Ringbom started the cultural center RIAC and later RIACFILMS in Dakar, organizing animation workshops in Senegal and other African countries (Figure D.2).

FIGURE D.1 Antonia Ringbom lives in Korppoo, in Turku archipelago, where she has built an animation studio. (With permission from Klaus Somerkoski for Firma Antonia Ringbom.)

In 2014, Ringbom was invited to run another workshop at the Luxor African Film Festival. The festival curator Mohammed Ghazala visited Korppoo as a guest of Finnanimation and became enthusiastic about Ringbom's cut-out style with animal characters colored in purple, pink, orange, and yellow. A few years later, I sat down for coffee in Berlinale with a guy who teaches animation in Alexandria. Couldn't be more delighted when the teacher showed me some student work from his computer, and surprisingly many of those resembled Ringbom's animations both in colors and

FIGURE D.2 *Yellow Giraffe's Animal Stories* (1997) got inspiration from trips to Africa by their creator Antonia Ringbom. The series with 26 episodes of 7-minute duration was produced by Mikael Wahlforss at the production company Epidem ZOT. It received the UNICEF prize and Silver Pulcinella for the Best Series in Europe in 1997. (With Permission from Epidem.)

themes with strong animal or female characters. I asked whether students have taken a trip to Luxor the year Ringbom's workshop took place. The teacher nodded, as the Finnish name had been in his memory. Ringbom was also interviewed for a local TV station surrounded by Sphinxes.

Ringbom has also made the title sequence for the feature *Moomin and the Comet Chase* (2010) accompanied by Icelandic Björk singing. *The Arkipellina* 29-minute short (2016) and series 26×7 (2018–2020) tell fantasy stories from the archipelago. Her other series *Mindscapes* (2017) has independent episodes, where the artist has given a voice to people with mental disabilities. The series has become a long-time favorite on the YLE Areena streaming service.

Ringbom was one of the Finnish–Swedish women who belonged to the so-called "Berit's Stable." Berit Neumann-Lund, who worked

FIGURE D.3 "Tjejmaffian" or The Girl Mafia was called a group of Finnish–Swedish illustrators who made animations for Svenska Yle—the Swedish language part of Finnish national broadcasting company. Their work was considered "the world's best," as they received many prizes in the early 1970s. (With permission from Camilla Mickwitz estate.)

as the head of the Finnish–Swedish children's department at YLE, arranged job opportunities for artistically gifted young women. Berit's method was learning by doing, and many team members became very successful (Figure D.3).

Camilla Mickwitz's animation *Jason's Summer* (1973) was named the world's best animation at the Hollywood Film & TV Festival. Mickwitz, who passed away in the middle of her career in 1989, is also known for animating the theme song for *Tiny Two (Pikku Kakkonen)*—the children's magazine program and the world's finest "beware of weak ice" warning video (*Heikot jäät: Varokaa heikkoa jäätä!*, 1986). Christina Andersson got the Prix

Jeunesse award for *Mats and His Parents (Mats och hans föräldrar,* 1972), which portrays the divorce from a child's point of view. A child wonders if his parents have to walk backwards out of the church, and if growing apart means that a father will turn into a giant (Leinonen, 2014, p. 135).

During the 100th anniversary year of Finnish animation in 2014, Berit and her team's work was highlighted in a TV documentary codirected by Antonia Ringbom and Pii Berg. Unfortunately, not so many of these unusual animations have been re-run on any Nordic TV channels due to copyright issues. "The Girl Mafia," as they were called, was dissolved as early as 1975 due to a crisis over fees. They were not allowed to work for free, even if they wanted to (Nylund, 2014).

When YLE first reduced and, in the early 1990s, stopped making animation in-house, it meant an outbreak of more Indie production companies. Epidem, although started as a documentary production company as early as 1968, had been a strong producer of animated shorts and series with directors such as Camilla Mickwitz, Jaana Wahlforss, and Marjut Rimminen since the late 1970s. Antonia Ringbom started her own company in Firma Antonia Ringbom in 1990.

Bettina Björnberg-Aminoff—the youngest attendee of Berit's Stable, born in 1962 in Nauvo, in the heart of the Finnish archipelago, but lived in Sweden through her childhood and youth, has been working with several production companies after her years on YLE. She started *Lalla & Mix* (2009) series with Leino Production, whereas the last six episodes were made at Långfilm. The series was supported by YLE with a presale, and the Finnish Film Foundation with its Production Support, additionally, provided a grant by The Swedish Cultural Foundation in Finland, being a very influential supporter of the Swedish-speaking minority in Finland with 38,000,000 total budget in 2020. (Finnish Film Foundation supported film production in 2020 with 21,526,399 Euros.)

Appendix E

NOMAD STORIES: Veronica Lassenius and Pikkukala

When Veronica Lassenius (b. 1975) received an annual grant from The Swedish Cultural Foundation in 2016, she decided to make an animated short about the fashion industry and the habit of overconsuming clothes. *A Long Story Short* (2017) discovers the origins of a t-shirt from cotton plantations, through the factories with interesting machines, into stores, and then to a child's wardrobe. The film explains how much freshwater or energy is needed for cotton to grow, and how much transportation between different places is required. The short is made in a funny cut-out style with colorful pieces of paper and different fabrics, but the topic of fast fashion and recycling has importance.

Veronica studied costume design in Paris. After her studies, she moved to Madrid and worked for a while for Canal+. She started Stor Fisk studio together with producer Pablo Jordi in Madrid, then moved to Barcelona. Stor Fisk produced *Saari* (2009) and *Fungi* (2012), both created and directed by Veronica Lassenius, in coproduction with Televisió de Catalunya.

In 2012, Veronica moved back to Finland with her family and founded Pikkukala Oy. The company produced *A Long Story Short*, launched books, apps for kids, and developed several

FIGURE E.1 *Royals Next Door* is the third series created by Veronica Lassenius but the first one produced by their Finnish company Pikkukala. (With permission of Pikkukala.)

TV series. In 2019, Pikkukala opened a studio in Barcelona. Pikkukala Barcelona got involved in international coproductions like *Stinky Dog*, and productions like *Royals Next Door*.

Royals Next Door (2021) is an animation series that originated in Pikkukala with coproducers from Spain, Belgium, and Ireland. The world premiere was on RTÉ2 in Ireland in December 2021, followed by YLE and RTVE (Figure E.1).

According to Veronica, in *Royals Next Door* she had wanted to express her own experiences on how it felt as a child when the family was moving around after her father's work. In the series, the monarchs have to leave the castle for an ordinary suburb. Princess Stella is only happy about moving to new places and a chance to live a regular life with school plays, sports practices, and cleaning the house.

The Irish coproducer on *Royals Next Door* is Tamsin Lyons from Ink & Light. Ink & Light has bases in both Ireland and

Finland—two countries of similar size and population size. Whereas, Ireland has been experiencing a huge boom in animation production over the past 10 years, Finland's growth has been more modest. But it seems that the situation is changing, Tamsin says. International students who weren't aware of Finnish animation previously are beginning to take note of the opportunities available in Finland to work on high-quality animation series and films in an international environment. That fresh influx of talent is crucial, alongside native Finnish artists with professional experience, for a long-term sustainable community and industry (Figure E.2).

FIGURE E.2 Finnish producers listening to Anttu Harlin giving a speech during the Finnish Spotlight in Cartoon Forum in 2018. From left Petteri Pasanen, Maija Arponen, Nick Dorra, Ulla Junell-Pulkkinen, Veronica Lassenius, Tamsin Lyons, Leevi Lemmetty, Jim Solatie, and Pia Solatie. (Courtesy of Cartoon.)

References

INTERVIEWS

Denmark:

A.Film + H.C.Andersen animations: Jorgen Lerdam (Jun 2021), Anders Mastrup (Jun 2022)
Copenhagen Bombay and Zentropa/Princess: Sarita Christensen (Jan 2022)
LEGO animations: Irene Sparre (June 2021) (Michael Hegner (Aug 2012) when lecturing in Hanasaari, Finland)
Viborg + Nørlum: Claus Toksvig Kjaer (June 2021)
Viborg + Late Love Productions: Lana Tankosa Nikolic (June 2021)

Finland:

Anima Vitae: Mikko Pitkänen (Jan 2021), Kari Juusonen (Feb 2021) (Antti Haikala and Petteri Pasanen commenting)
Ferly: Ulla Junell-Pulkkinen (Jan 2021), Leena Fredriksson (Jan 2021), Joonas Risssanen + Meruan Salim (Sept 2019)
Gigglebug Entertainment: Genevieve Dexter (Feb 2021) Orion Ross 5/2021, Anttu *Harlin* (Sept 2021)
Gutsy + Moomins: Marika Makaroff (Feb 2021), Virpi Immonen (Mar 2021), Miiko Toi-viainen (May 2021), Jarmo Lampela (May 2021), Harri Roto (July 2021), Tom Devlin (Sept 2019)
Rovio: Tom van Waveren (Feb 2021), Mikko Pöllä (Feb 2021), Mikael Hed (Jun 2021) (Nick Dorra comments)
Pikkuli: Metsämarja Aittokoski (Mar 2021)
Others: Mikko Kunnas (Jan 2021), Timo-Pekko Nieminen (Feb 2021), Petri Kemppinen, (Aug 2021), Tuula Leinonen (Nov 2021).

Iceland:

Caoz: Arnar Gunnarson 6/2021
GunHil: Gunnar Karlssson and Hilmar Sigurðsson 6/2021

Norway:

Troll Film: Anita Killi 6/2021 (Lillian Løvseth and Sanne Augusta Løkke commenting)

Kool Produktion + General: Frank Mosvold 6/2021

Qvisten Animation + Nordic Christmas: Rasmus A. Sivertsen and Ove Heiborg 6/2021

Titina, Mikrofilms: Lise Fearnley 2/2022 (Tonje Skar Reiersen comments)

General: Kristine Knudsen: 12/2022

(Ivo Caprino: Remo Caprino 6/2022 comments)

Sweden:

Happy Life Animation: Torbjorn Jansson 6/2021 (Magnus Carlsson comments 5/2022)

General: Ingrid Edström 10/2021, Johan Edström 6/2021 + 10/2021

Sluggerfilm and Metropia: Christian Ryltenius 7/2021 (Mikael

LEE Film, Stockholm: Linda Hambäck 6/2021

(Johan Hagelback 1/2017)

Nomad stories:

Veronica Wallenberg 7/2021, Virpi Kettu 1/2021

Moscow: Marko Röhr and Janne Kopu 2010

Tallinn: Kati Kovacs 2/2021, Sanni Lahtinen, Heta Jääliinoja + Joni Männistö 3/2021

Antonia Ringbom, Veronica Lassenius, Pablo Jordi, Tamsin Lyons just comments 5/2022.

BOOKS AND ARTICLES

General

Aurell, Brontë, *The Little Book of Scandi Living*, White Lion Publishing, London, United Kingdom, 2020.

Barrett, Clive, *The Viking Gods: Pagan Myths of Nordic Peoples*, HarperCollins, England, 1989.

Bendazzi, Giannalberto, *Cartoons One Hundred Years of Cinema Animation*, Indiana University Press, 1994.

Bendazzi, Giannalberto, *Animation: A World History Volume I: Foundations - The Golden Age*, Routledge, 2015.

Brandon, Ruth, *Surreal Lives, The Surrealists 1917–1945*, Macmillan, New York, 1999.

Dee, Michael, *Ett nätverk av oändlig talang, Monitor Magazine*, July 6, 2021.

Faber, Liz, and Walters, Helen, *Animation Unlimited Innovative Short Films Since 1940*, Laurence King Publishing, 2004.

Foster, Elizabeth, *What's Behind the Spike in Popularity for Nordic Content*, Kidscreen, November 10, 2020.

Greene, Andy, et al., *The 100 Greatest Music Videos. From Adele to ZZ Top — our ranked list of the best music videos of all time*. Rolling Stone, Paranoid Android section, 2011. Available at: https://au.rollingstone.com/music/music-lists/best-music-videos-28407/radiohead-paranoid-android-28490/.

Ida Moen, Johnson, *The Barn and the Beast: The Queerness of Child-Animal Figurations in Scandinavian Literature and Culture*, University of California, Berkeley, 2020.

Keslassy, Elsa, *Animation Business in Scandinavia Entices Distributors Looking Alternatives to U.S. Fare*, Variety, February 28, 2014.

Pikkov, Ülo, *Animasophy – Theoretical Writings on the Animated Film*, Estonian Academy of Arts, 2010.

Pontieri, Laura, *Soviet Animation and the Thaw of the 1960s – Not Only for Children*, New Barnet, John Libbey Publishing Ltd, 2012.

Read, Herbert, *A Concise History of Modern Painting*, Thames and Hudson, London, 1986.

Robinson, Chris, *Unsung Heroes of Animation*, John Libbey Publishing, United Kingdom, 2006.

Sarane, Alexandrian, *Surrealist Art*, Thames and Hudson, London, 1970.

Sedgqick, Marcus, *Iceland from Thor to Odin: A Guide to the Norse Gods*, Guardian, February 4, 2015.

Tyree, Wynne, *Dealing with the Pandemic 'Peer-Ent' Shift*, Kidscreen, October 20, 2021.

Valk, Ülo, Sävborg, Daniel and Arukask, Madis, *Storied and Supernatural Places: Studies in Spatial and Social Dimensions of Folklore and Sagas*, Finnish Literature Society (SKS), 2018.

Vähäkylä, Liisa, *Pohjoismaisella yhteistyöllä vahvempaa animaatiovientiä*, AVEK Magazine, 2018.

WeAnimate Magazines, All Issues, All Articles, 2018–2022. www.nordicanimation.com

Denmark

Brewer, Jenny, *Animated Children's TV Show about a Man with a Long and Multifunctional Penis Debuts in Denmark*, https://www.itsnicethat.com/news/john-dillermand-jacob-ley-dr-animation-070121, January 7, 2021.

Film #46 Special Issue/Animation, September 2005.

Ikonen, Niko, *Ternet Ninja Tanskan katsotuin elokuva vuosikymmeniin on animaatio – mutta ei lapsille suunnattu sellainen. Jotain sen viehätyksestä saattaa jäädä siirtymättä kulttuurirajojen yli*. Episodi, 2019, https://www.episodi.fi/elokuvat/ternet-ninja.

Jokinen, Heikki, *The Long Shadow Over The Atlantic*, AWN, January 1, 1999.

Plaschke, Niels, *Nye tider i dansk tegnefilm*, in *Dansk tegnefilm gennem 100 år*, edited by Annemette Karpen, 2008.

Rasmussen, Jonas Poher and Nawabi, Amin, *Flee – Animated Documentary Puts a Human Face on the Faraway Plight of Refugees*, Original Cin, December 16, 2021.

Villon, Rebekah, *The BIG Picture: Sarita Christensen and Copenhagen Bombay,* WeAnimate Magazine, 2021.

Walmer, Nathan, *Culture Round-Up Danish-French Film Takes Home Cartoon World's Answer to the Oscars,* The Copenhagen Post, June 25, 2020.

Finland

Ahola, Suvi, *Towards The Empty Page,* Books from Finland, https://kansallisbiografia.fi/english/person/1395, Issue 3/1991.

Bandler, Vivica and Backström, Carita, *Vastaanottaja tuntematon,* Finnish Translation Juha Siltanen, Otava, Finland, 1992.

Dudok de Wit, Alex, *Royals Next Door Breaks New Ground for Finnish (And European) Animation,* www.cartoonbrew.com, 2020.

Gartz, Juho, *Animaatioelokuvat,* SES julkaisusarja, No. 6, 1978.

Happonen, Sirke, *Vilijonkka ikkunassa – Tove Janssonin muumiteosten kuva, sana ja liike,* WSOY, Porvoo, 2007.

Holländer, Tove, *Fron Idyll to non-idyll, An Analysis of the Illustrations in Tove Jansson's Moomin Books,* Publications of the Finnish Institute for Children's Literature, 4, 1983.

Honkanen, Jenni, *Al-Jazeera vie Pikkulin yli sataan maahan,* TS, April 26, 2018.

Jansson, Tove, *Kirjeenvaihtoa,* in *Viesti – valitut novellit 1971–1997,* translated from Swedish to Finnish by Oili Suominen, WSOY, Helsinki, 1999.

Jansson, Tove, *Kuvitteluleikki,* in collection Muumit sarjakuvaklassikot II, translated from Swedish to Finnish by Anita Salmivuori and Juhani Tolvanen WSOY, Helsinki, orig. Moominmamma's Maid, Evening News, 1956.

Jones, W., Glyn, *Tove Jansson,* Twayne's World Authors Series, Scandinavian Literature, Twayne Publishers, Boston, 1984.

Kuorikoski, Juha, *Pelien Suomi: Tarinoita kotimaiselta pelialalta,* Gaudeamus, 2021.

Lamppu, Eva, *Big in Japan, But Could America Love Moomin?,* Reuter, October 5, 2009.

Lee Tahnak, Jeana, *Leading Chinese Animation Studio Crimson Forest to Bring Legendary Finnish Mythology to Life,* Business Wire, September 29, 2011.

Leinonen, Tuula, *100 vuotta suomalaista animaatiota,* AALTO Arts Books, Helsinki, 2014.

Lewin, Alyssa, *Joining Niko on Its Way to the Stars, Nordic Children's Films Ability to Reach a Wider Audience,* Biografcentralen, Report 2013:1.

Niskanen, Eija, *Muumibrändi Japanissa, Animaatioala Suomessa vuonna 2010,* Finnanimation.

Raeste, Juha-Pekka, *Tuotteista taiteeksi, Muumien toimitusjohtaja kertoo strategiamuutoksesta,* HS Teema, 2, 2013.

Römpötti Harri, *Björk valitsi muumit jo pikkutyttönä,* HS, August 3, 2010.

Römpötti Harri, *Momolu-panda matkaa maailmalle,* Suomen Kuvalehti, 23/2019.

Tuchow, Ryan, *Cool New Shows - Royals Next Door,* Kidscreen, October, 2020.

Tuchow, Ryan, *'Tis (still) the Season,* Kidscreen, July/August, 2020.

Vähäkylä, Liisa, *Etelä-Korea ostaa ja myy hahmoja,* HS August 12, 2011.

Vähäkylä, Liisa and Pulkkis, Nina, *Muumeista Miljoonabisnes,* Siltala, 2017.

Iceland

Fantasy
Rosser, Michael, *Belgian's Cyborn Joins Animated 'Ploey You Never Fly Alone'*, Screen Daily, May 23, 2015.

Norway

Anon, *Video: Ewok-like Creatures Chilling in Krabi Cave Turn Out to be Performance Art Piece*, coconuts.co/bangkok/news, November 6, 2018.
Anon, *Impact of the Norwegian Film Incentive*, A Report to the Norwegian Film Institute from Olsberg SPI, January 13, 2017.
Villon, Rebekah, https://weanimate.dk/bingo-how-determination-made-a-nordic-kids-franchise/?utm_source=linkedin&utm_medium=social&utm_campaign=ReviveOldPost
Bingo! – How Determination Made a Nordic Kids Franchise, WeAnimate Magazine, 2021.
NAAM YAI – Tori Wrånes, 2018. https://www.toriwraanes.com/naam-yai
Parker, Martin and Kajsa Næss, (1970). https://www.nordicwomeninfilm.com/person/kajsa-naess/, Petersen, Jens, Aftonbladet.
Reschefski, Lisa, *Staying True to Astrid Lindgren*, WA Magazine.
Simon, Ben, *Pinchcliffe Races Home: A Look Back At Caprino Studios*, Retrospectives/March 20, 2006.
Skinner, Toby, *A Very Flåklypa Christmas*, June 13, 2017/July 19, 2018.
Strøm, Gunnar, *Der blomstrar som aldrig förr Norsk animations historia och nutid*, Animagi, 1955.
Strøm, Gunnar, *Mannen som ble Norges Disney*, https://www.aftenposten.no/meninger/kronikk/i/GGbwoV/mannen-som-ble-norges-disney-gunnar-stroem Aftenposten, 2020.

Sweden

Andersson, Lars Gustaf, *A History of Swedish Experimental Film Culture: From Early Animation to Video Art*, John Libbey Publishing, National Library of Sweden, Indiana University Press, 2010.
Animagi: tidskrift om animation, Konstfack, Institutionen för animation & animerad film, 2003–2004.
Film Studies: An International Review, Description: nr.1(1999)–2(2000), 8(2006)–11(2007).
Gessaen, Nasha, *The Fifteen-Year-Old Climate Activist Who Is Demanding a New Kind of Politics*, New Yorker, https://www.newyorker.com/news/our-columnists/the-fifteen-year-old-climate-activist-who-is-demanding-a-new-kind-of-politics, October 2, 2018.
Gustafsson, Tommy, *Det var en Gång, Historia för barn I svensk television under det långa 1970-talet*, Universus Academic Press, Malmö, 2014.

204 ■ References

Katalog från utställningen, *Kapten Grogg och hans vänner*, 1989, Innehåller en artikel om Bergdahl på sid 347, 1916,537 st animationsceller från "Den fatal konserten i Cirkus Fjollinski, 1916.

Kenyon, Heather, *Since September*, AWN, January 1, 2001.

Marko-Nord, Adam and Claes Jurander, *Om Animation*, Göteborg, 2002.

Marko-Nord, Adam, *Den svenska animationsbranschen: en rapport*, Svenska Filminstitutet, 2005.

Petterson, Åsa, *TV For Children How Swedish Public Service Television Imagines A Child Audience*, Linköping Studies in Arts and Science No. 583, 2013, Linköping University, Department of Thematic Studies Linköping, 2013.

Robinson, Chris, *The Spectacular Hi-Fi/Low-Fi Sounds and Images of Studio FilmTecknarna*, AWN, October 29, 2001.

Sonesson, Inga, *Förskolebarn och TV*, Scandinavian University Books, Esselte Studium, 1979.

Whittingham, Clive, *TV4 hires Veteran Gustafsson For Scripted*, C21 Media, June 24, 2020.

Index

Note: **Bold** page numbers refer to tables; *italic* page numbers refer to figures.

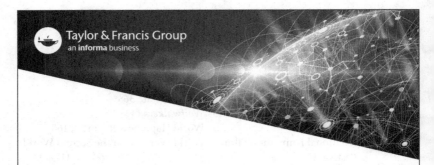

Printed in the United States
by Baker & Taylor Publisher Services

Printed in the United States
by Baker & Taylor Publisher Services